$PLAN

$ELL

$PEAK TO $ELL

PERSUADE, INFLUENCE, AND ESTABLISH AUTHORITY

& Promote Your Products, Services, Practice, Business, or Cause

The Science of Selling One-to-Many Instead of Many-to-One

By One Of America's Greatest Platform Salesmen

DAN KENNEDY

Advantage®

Published by Advantage, Charleston, South Carolina.
Member of Advantage Media Group.

ADVANTAGE is a registered trademark and the Advantage colophon is a trademark of Advantage Media Group, Inc.

Printed in the United States of America.

ISBN: 978-1-59932-771-6
LCCN: 2016939339

Book design by George Stevens.

This publication is designed to provide accurate and authoritative information in regard to the subject matter covered. It is sold with the understanding that the publisher is not engaged in rendering legal, accounting, or other professional services. If legal advice or other expert assistance is required, the services of a competent professional person should be sought.

Advantage Media Group is proud to be a part of the Tree Neutral® program. Tree Neutral offsets the number of trees consumed in the production and printing of this book by taking proactive steps such as planting trees in direct proportion to the number of trees used to print books. To learn more about Tree Neutral, please visit **www.treeneutral.com.** To learn more about Advantage's commitment to being a responsible steward of the environment, please visit **www.advantagefamily.com/green**

Advantage Media Group is a publisher of business, self-improvement, and professional development books. We help entrepreneurs, business leaders, and professionals share their Stories, Passion, and Knowledge to help others Learn & Grow. Do you have a manuscript or book idea that you would like us to consider for publishing? Please visit **advantagefamily.com** or call **1.866.775.1696.**

Dedicated to my fellow road warrior sales speakers with whom I have been privileged to share so many platforms and an era: Zig Ziglar, Jim Rohn, Brian Tracy and Tom Hopkins

CONTENTS

About the Author

 **DAN. S. KENNEDY** is a multi-millionaire, serial entrepreneur; trusted marketing advisor; famous consultant and coach; author of the popular No BS book series; accomplished sales professional; and well-respected and dynamic speaker. He influences over a million independent business owners through his coaching programs, newsletters, and group meetings across the country.

Dan has spoken to audiences as large as 35,000 and averaged an annual audience of over 250,000 for more than ten years. He has also shared the speaking stage with a collection of celebrity-entrepreneurs, ranging from Gene Simmons (KISS) and Zig Ziglar to Donald Trump and four former US presidents. On the Peter Lowe SUCCESS Tour, he averaged a higher dollar-per-audience member sales result than any other speaker in the history of the tour. Dan lives in Ohio and in northern Virginia with his wife, Carla, and their Million-Dollar Dog.

Don't Skip It. Read This First.

My friend, client, and *Book The Business* coauthor, Adam Witty, founder of the Advantage Media Group empire, asked me to write an utterly candid book about speaking-to-sell. As you may know, Advantage (advantagefamily.com) represents over a thousand top authorities, experts, and thought leaders in business, finance, medicine, and law around the globe. Many of them want to speak-to-sell, and Adam knew I could lend considerable expertise to the topic. I cautioned him: be careful what you wish for! This is the result.

In this book, I am going to lay out *exactly* what is required to stand up in front of an audience of twenty, two hundred, two thousand, or twenty thousand and deliver a purpose-driven presentation that elicits the response you want—whether that is the immediate stampede to the back of the room to buy information products or register for a program; hurry to book appointments to meet with you; make donations to your church's building fund or charity's new initiative; or more "gently" embrace ideas, information, or advice you advocate. Whether you want to open and change minds or open wallets and extract money, this book tells you the unvarnished truth about how to do it.

Before you listen to anybody about anything, you should verify that they know what the devil they're talking about—based on personal, successful experience.

WHY LISTEN TO ME, ABOUT THIS?

Okay, the "America's Greatest Platform Salesman" tag on the book cover may be an overstatement. So shoot me.

The late, great Zig Ziglar said that I might be the best he's ever seen, and that's something, considering Zig pioneered the art and science of speaking-to-sell, sending stampedes to his back-of-room and floor-of-stadium product tables for five decades. Zig and I were on the number-one public seminar/event tour together for nine consecutive years. He saw me work. He saw my results. We compared results. He was not idly flattering me with his gracious comment.

I have *personally* sold well over $150 million in audio programs, courses, seminars, coaching programs, and assorted goods and services by standing on stage and speaking to thousands or tens of thousands, by standing at the front of small rooms speaking to dozens or hundreds, and even by standing in living rooms and speaking to a few, and by doing much the same thing via live webcasts and recorded webinars and speeches and presentations recorded on CDs and DVDs sent through the mail. I've sold from the stage to chiropractors, dentists, lawyers, restaurant owners, financial services professionals, carpet cleaners, funeral directors, golf course superintendents, Honda dealership service managers, members of the National Guild of Hypnotists, and even my own peers—authors, speakers, and publishers. For nine years, Zig and I were the only two speakers appearing on every one of the twenty-five to twenty-seven

SUCCESS events a year, held mostly in sports arenas and convention centers, with audiences of 10,000 to 35,000, where I sold over a million dollars of my products each year. I *know* a magic trick: how to pick pockets from a distance, en masse. (Note: if that description disturbs you, you are going to have a rough time with this book, but it confirms that you really need it.)

Maybe more importantly, I've turned countless people into powerful presenters and platform sales pros who never before spoke or who were speaking but failing miserably at selling from the stage. I've fixed 'em and created 'em from scratch. And I've devised group sales presentations for everything from Mace pepper spray to $50,000 franchises to MUA (Manipulation Under Anesthesia) chiropractic procedures to investment services. I've launched and built and helped clients launch and build multi-million-dollar businesses with group presentations delivered in seminars or via tele-seminars, webinars, and DVDs sent through the mail. I've been at this since 1975.

It is vital to understand that there is a Grand Canyon-sized difference between "speaking" and "speaking-to-sell." They have commonalities in the way that zebras and horses, football and soccer, steak and canned dog food, and water and Scotch have commonalities. Some ingredients or elements are the same or nearly the same. There are genealogical and genetic commonalities. Yet they are as different as can be, and the devil is in the differences. So, this book is not about speaking per se or its closest cousins: teaching, lecturing, entertaining, or motivating. It is not about being popular or beloved, it is not about applause and standing ovations, and it is not about peer approval or awards. It is about getting results and getting money. **My applause *is* money.** So, yes, personally, I have been a "professional speaker" since 1975, and I have spoken for association, corporate, information marketers', and seminar promoters' audiences in every kind of venue, by myself for days or alongside an incredibly diverse array of other professional speakers, thought leaders, celebrities, and political leaders. But unlike many professional speakers, I have never gone just for a fee and applause; I have always gone to get money from my audiences (as well as the client) at that moment and/or to round up customers to get money from and keep getting money from in the future. In doing so, I built a business worth more than $30 million, built a platform that birthed other businesses and companies—one worth over $200 million—and created ongoing income streams de-linked from speaking, although that is not the subject of this book. But I want you to understand that one of the ways I view and have used speaking-to-sell is as customer and client acquisition media and opportunity rather than as an isolated act or a "gig" or "job."

There is a *science* to all this. Some people take to it like ducks to water or woodchucks to wood-chucking or Kardashians to self-promotion. Others, frankly, find it difficult to get good enough at it for their purposes. But anybody can do it because there is a *science* to it. However, the mechanics are not enough. Even if you know them, fully understand them, and accept them conceptually, if your own mind-set, emotional makeup, personal vulnerability to criticism, or other internal "issues" are not made compatible with all the mechanics needed to be successful, success will not come. How you decide to think and feel about what I lay out for you here will have far more impact on your success than what you know and understand about speaking-to-sell from this book. It is a stomach-churning cliché to say that "attitude governs altitude," but in this case it is absolutely true—not (just) an optimistic and confident attitude, though, but a relatively unusual, clear, somewhat ruthless attitude about results and about why you are there and a refusal to sacrifice or even compromise that result for any other agenda.

ONE-TO-MANY INSTEAD OF ONE-TO-ONE

Everybody should use this, one way or another, for the simple reason of speed. Selling one-to-one is inefficient. Selling—or at least sifting and sorting great prospects worth meeting with one-to-one from poor prospects best tossed back in the lake—one-to-many is very efficient. In the same hour that it takes to tell your story to one prospect across desk or kitchen table, you can tell it to ten, a hundred, or a thousand. An hour divided by ten equals an investment of just six minutes per prospect. An hour divided by a hundred equals an investment of just six seconds per prospect.

You don't get this kind of marketing or sales efficiency for free. It has its price.

Most such efficiency can be bought with your checkbook. As I write this, you can buy a good month's run of direct-response radio commercials on Rush Limbaugh for about $250,000 to $500,000. You'll be heard by an avid, responsive audience of ten million or more, on over 850 radio stations in nearly that many local markets. If you divide $250,000 by 850, you are investing only $294 in each market, which would get you nearly nothing if offered to any one of those stations directly. You are getting great sales efficiency and rented, transferred authority and influence for these dollars.

Using speaking, you rarely (also) open up your checkbook. Often you get paid. But the sales efficiency of speaking to audiences still carries price tags. Two of them. One is learning, practicing, getting good at, and adhering to the practical mechanics, presentation architecture, and presentation skills that are required. That surprises few. It's likely why you procured this book. But the second price tag—not second in importance—is reengineering your attitude, view of self, view of business, view of world around you, and thoughts and emotions (to whatever extent necessary) in order to be effective.

A RICH TRADITION

Selling one-to-many dates, here in America, to the turn of the last century, with traveling "medicine men," as seen in several classic musicals or represented by the iconic and infamous Dr. John Brinkley, subject of the book I coauthored with Chip Kessler, *Making Them Believe*, which I would encourage you to get and read.

It is also rooted in party plan selling, which took America by storm during the post–World War II boom and rise of suburbia. This, of course, lives on today, with great companies like Tupperware conducting in-home parties every night in over twenty countries around the globe. Harley-Davidson uses "garage parties" to sell motorcycles to women. When Botox first came on the scene, many doctors did Botox® home parties hosted by patients in their living rooms. I once owned an interest in a thriving company that took the home party (tweaked to "crime safety class") into company, hospital, real estate office, etc. break rooms, there to sell chemical deterrents on key chains and other personal defense products, averaging $300 to $500 in sales per small class, enabling "instructors" working part time to earn upward of $1,000 a week, $50,000 a year. I've helped implant dentists, cosmetic dentists, cosmetic surgeons, financial advisors, banks, and even restaurants create in-office or in-store "parties" or classes to sell. In my book, *No BS Guide to Maximum Referrals*, one of the guest expert chapters is from Susie Nelson, one of the leading experts and business coaches in the party-plan industry, making the case for every business utilizing party-plan selling.

The multilevel-marketing industry, rising rapidly at the same time—its greatest boom in the United States was from 1950 to 1980, and early on featured companies like Nutri-Bio, Nutrilite, and Shaklee, then Amway, Bestline, and its cousins, the ultimately outlawed pyramid selling giants like Holiday Magic, Koscot, and Dare to Be Great—shared the in-home "opportunity meeting" roots, but most moved to larger hotel meetings in time. This American invention spread throughout the globe. It also birthed a lot of well-known professional speakers, including Zig, Jim Rohn, and me, to name three. The "opportunity meeting"—in living rooms with ten, hotel ballrooms with a hundred or a thousand, or transferred to TV broadcast (as Herbalife did), infomercial, DVD, or webcast—is a dynamic, well-proven model for speaking-to-sell.

The "free preview seminar" became the predominate means of selling "how to get rich in real estate" (thanks to Al Lowry Jr.) in the 1960s through the 1980s—and continues to this day, with traveling "preview speakers" working rooms filled by the old standby of big newspaper ads as well as radio spots, TV infomercials, direct mail, and online marketing. Today, some of these touring sales teams are linked to reality TV stars. Over the years, this modus operandi has been borrowed and profitably used to sell many things: other kinds of business opportunities and franchises, financial planning and wealth management services, health products like juicers and home therapy pools, security systems, and on and on. More B2B, I created a company that, in its prime four years (1983 to 1987), put over 18,000 chiropractic physicians, dentists, podiatrists, and veterinarians into three-hour evening preview seminars, directly selling over $8 million in educational programs, plus "back-end," additional training, advertising media, and other services. That *exact* model for filling such seminars and selling educational resources to private-practice professionals, other business owners, and sales professionals is used by several of my clients right now or has recently been used to launch or expand an existing enterprise, and in 2014, in total, created over $50 million directly for my clients and fueled ten times that much to boot. Turned into an "executive briefing" and held during the day instead of in evenings, it sells software, other business equipment, agency services, and consulting.

I say that selling one-to-many has a *rich tradition* not just because it has deep roots and is as American as apple pie and Roy Rogers but also because its worth as a marketing methodology is incalculable, as it has created so much wealth for so many people and companies. More importantly, that tradition, those roots, and all the experience it represents has provided very reliable, formulaic models for success.

The speaker selling pamphlets, books, and courses from the stage dates back, at least, to Mark Twain and P.T. Barnum, authors like Napoleon Hill, and the pioneers of "professional platform selling" like J. Douglas Edwards, Zig Ziglar, Cavett Robert (founder of the National Speakers Association), and many others. These men were—for a time or for their entire lives—essentially traveling salesmen, akin to door-to-door encyclopedia salesmen but knocking on five hundred doors and selling to five hundred prospects per hour instead of one.

FROM BASIC TO MOST SOPHISTICATED

Selling one-to-many has fueled and continues to fuel the direct-selling industry, the multi-level/network-marketing industry, the "get rich" training industry, information marketing in many niches, and many local businesses with owners smart enough to use it—from dental practices to gardening centers to financial advisors—at a basic level. However, the same methodology is relied on in much more sophisticated environments. IPOs are assembled in Wall Street skyscrapers by highly skilled pitchmen making group presentations to potential underwriters and investment firms. Ad agencies secure accounts with boardroom pitch presentations. Committees are audiences. If you watch the ABC show *Shark Tank*, you can see how being good or clumsy or awful at making a pitch to a committee plays out.

It's hard to imagine a person or a business that can't benefit from its spokesperson knowing how to sell one-to-many and from devising or securing opportunities to do so.

THIS BOOK IS....

A condensation of my forty years of speaking for my supper, eating what I killed in an audience that day, and rounding up herds providing future meals. I no longer rely on this for my daily meals, but I still do it on occasion because of its unrivaled combination of efficiency and effectiveness. I still, often, guide clients into utilizing one-to-many selling, via different means. This book is unsweetened; it tells, to the best of my knowledge, how to do it and how to screw it up, why some excel and others flop, and what is *required* of the speaker who sells. It is all about the Benjamins, and I won't keep qualifying that—for the record, I presume you are selling something legitimately beneficial that you believe in, therefore no squeamishness or apology for doing so as persuasively as possible is warranted. And, for the record, if you can't come to this with a conviction that no apology is warranted for the selling part, you are doomed.

If you can speak-to-sell, you need never go hungry—unless lost in an entirely unpopulated forest or jungle (which, as a bonus piece of advice, I suggest avoiding). If you can devise one-to-many selling opportunities, you can grow your business faster and more efficiently than your competitors and target and connect with ideal prospects and clients no one else will reach. People often ask me: if you had to start over tomorrow, knowing what you know now but pretty much devoid of resources, how would you get going? This book is my answer.

Some of the Notable Authors, Speakers, Business Leaders, and Celebrities Dan Kennedy Has Appeared With as a Speaker

Political and World Leaders

President Ronald Reagan*

President Gerald Ford*

President George Bush*

Gen. Norm Schwarzkopf*

Secretary Colin Powell*

Lady Margaret Thatcher*

Celebrity Entrepreneurs

Donald Trump

Ivanka Trump

George Ross (The Trump Organization)*

Debbi Fields (Mrs. Fields Cookies)*

Ben & Jerry (Ben & Jerry's Ice Cream)

Gene Simmons (KISS)

Joan Rivers

Kathy Ireland

Kevin O'Leary (*Shark Tank*)

Entertainment Celebrities

Naomi Judd*

Johnny Cash

Mary Tyler Moore*

Christopher Reeve*

The Smothers Brothers

John Rich

Broadcasters

Larry King*

Paul Harvey*

Deborah Norville

Barbara Walters

Sports Personalities

Joe Montana*

Troy Aikman*

Peyton Manning*

Emmitt Smith

George Foreman*

Muhammad Ali*

Mary Lou Retton*

Coach Jimmy Johnson*

Coach Lou Holtz*

Authors and Speakers

Zig Ziglar*

Brian Tracy*

Jim Rohn*

Tom Hopkins*

Tony Robbins*

Mark Victor Hansen (Chicken Soup for the Soul)*

Nido Qubein (President, High Point University)*

Loral Langemeir**

Mike Vance (Dean, Disney University)*

Michael Gerber (E-Myth)

Marketing and Direct Marketing Leaders and Master Copywriters

Gary Halbert*

John Carlton*

Brian Kurtz*

Jay Abraham*

Jim McCann (1-800-Flowers)

Joe Sugarman (Blu-Blockers)*

Newsmakers

Lt. Col. Oliver North

Gerry Spence*

Alan Dershowitz*

Ian Calder (National Enquirer)

Events and Organizations

SUCCESS (234 Events)

Titans of Direct Marketing

Direct Marketing Association

Parker Chiropractic Convention

Excellence in Dentistry

American Writers & Artists

Over 200 Other Niche Industry Conferences

Infusionsoft Multi-City Tours

Appeared with on multiple occasions

"My friend Dan Kennedy is unique, a genius in many ways. I have always admired his ability to see the vital truths in any business and to state these realities with straight language and clear definitions. His approach is direct. His ideas are controversial. His ability to get results for his clients is unchallenged."

BRIAN TRACY

America's foremost personal development speaker

"By Dan Kennedy's direct guidance, I went from being a popular and busy speaker with a modest income and virtually no ability to sell from the platform to earning over $1 million in the next two years from platform sales—a transformation."

FOSTER HIBBARD

For twenty years, one of the most revered and popular speakers to the chiropractic profession. A former personal associate of Napoleon Hill.

"It is thanks to Dan that I totally understand the difference between speaking and speaking-to-sell and to move people to action. I have used that knowledge to sell millions of dollars of resources and coaching programs from the stage."

LEE MILTEER

Author, Reclaim the Magic

CHAPTER 1

The Best Way to Make a Lot of Money in an Hour, without a Gun

Robbing banks has its pluses and minuses. I know a somewhat famous entrepreneur who once successfully robbed six banks in one day via the principle of delegation and got away with it . . . the first time. But he wound up with tattoos and a habit of sitting with his back against the wall. It didn't work out well the second time.

Speaking-to-sell has its pluses and minuses, too. It *is* possible to pick the wrong thing to sell and do it well and also wind up with tattoos and a habit of sitting with your back against the wall. I know a couple guys in that fraternity. But for most businesspeople, it can be the best way to make a lot of money in an hour, without a gun and without any significant risk of incarceration or death. This is why you have to very seriously scheme to put one-to-many selling, by personal speaking as well as by other means, to work for yourself or your business. Frankly, *not* doing so is foolish.

Ron Popeil, an inventor, did what few inventors are ever willing to do: go out and sell his products personally, by standing up on folding chairs, soapboxes, and stages, to perfect the pitches transferred into one-to-many selling by media. This is the road to riches traveled by Ron as well as Jay Kordich (a.k.a. The Juiceman, aided by my friend Rick Cesari, author of the book *Buy Now*) and many other millionaires and multi-millionaires. My own *Magnetic Marketing System's*® sales letters used by my companies, Nightingale-Conant, and others to sell thousands and thousands of courses at $278 to $499 came from transcriptions of the several versions of the speech that sold even more, perfected in small rooms and from large stages. Inventors love telling potential investors about their product, but it's infinitely more persuasive to prove that you have a perfected pitch that sells like crazy. Speaking is the best way to work out a pitch transferable to other media and leverageable to a fortune.

A giant company like Amway, begun by two guys in a rented, out-of-business gas station—two guys who became billionaires, one the owner of the Orlando Magic NBA team—was *built on the strength of a single speech*, the Opportunity Presentation, fondly thought of by insiders as "the drawing of the circles." That little speech, concocted and perfected by Rich and Jay, has been delivered in millions of living rooms over about sixty years, taken shy and frightened and poor people and made them high-income businesspeople, and fueled a global multibillion-dollar empire. Mr. Gamble of Proctor & Gamble famously said, "Any fool can make soap. It takes a genius to sell it." I wonder what he would think of the little Amway opportunity talk heard daily and nightly 'round the world that has sold more soap than any ad campaign ever conceived by other manufacturers. Because of the unique nature of multilevel marketing, that little speech, given to four couples in an apartment's living room, can wind up making the person delivering it a million dollars. By the way, I can still draw the circles and deliver this speech, even though the last time I did it was in 1974. Hand me the chalk and look out. And you might be surprised to know how many top business leaders who use one-to-many, structured sales presentations in other businesses once held that chalk and drew those circles, and learned much that they do today from the experience. Bill Guthy, cocreator of the multibillion-dollar infomercial-driven company Guthy-Renker Corporation comes to mind.

My client Dr. Chris Tomshack perfected his own "Discovery Day"—a daylong speech that sells—and took a fledgling company from 4 to 360+ franchised clinics at a speed unheard of in franchising, in less than thirty-six months. My friend Matt Zagula is able to earn a seven-figure income as a financial advisor in a small, blue-collar West Virginia town because he can stand up in front of groups and convince them to hand over their life savings to his management. (He and I coauthored the book *No BS Guide to Trust-Based Marketing: Creating Trust in an Understandably Un-Trusting World*.) My occasional client Lisa Miller gets major hospitals under contract to her firm, for cost reduction and containment consulting, with her compensation based on percentage of uncovered savings—such contracts often worth hundreds of thousands of dollars each—because she has a structured sales speech that she can convincingly deliver to small groups of hospital executives. All possible because of "The Pitch" and the ability to deliver it by speaking.

At the local level, I've worked with very diverse speak-to-sell situations. The restaurant owner who put over two hundred customers into a monthly auto-charge membership, locking in over $30,000 of certain monthly income by speaking to groups, and by speaking-to-sell that membership to customers invited to dinner meetings. The dentist who books over 50% of his office's business for the month with one evening seminar about implant dentistry held the first Thursday of each month, by speaking-to-sell. The travel agent prospering in a dying industry, by speaking-to-sell luxury cruises. This varied list is long.

Speaking-to-sell sharpens you. It makes you better at communicating by every other means. It compels perfecting a persuasive sales story. It teaches you to structure and organize presentations. It builds skills, confidence, and power. It can also liberate you from selling to one person at a time, thereby being an income multiplier of great impact. It may allow you to duplicate yourself: if you have a winning presentation and learn to deliver it effectively, you can teach others to deliver it. But regardless of what, if any, long-term use you make of speaking-to-sell, the doing of it will sharpen you and your effectiveness at just about everything else you do. It may be the best "success education" there is.

By the way, there's a businessman who I've done a lot of business with over the years, who thinks I don't know he looks down on me, feels superior to me, and behind my back indicates as much because he went to college and I didn't. His college education had him stuck in a profitable business he disliked more with each passing year, getting up every morning and dutifully reporting to work as a worker. It's *my* education that first revolutionized that business of his and then liberated him from it, took him from local to global, led him to prominence and effectiveness as a speaker and a speaker who sells, as well as an author who hit the bestseller lists, and ultimately placed an enormous amount of wealth in his bank account and freedom in his hands. *My* education didn't come from professors on pleasant campuses. *My* education came from the street, selling to eat, learning the power and process and skill of speaking-to-sell in apartment living rooms and tiny Holiday Inn meeting rooms.

I mean no disrespect to college education, nor to anyone's pride from having matriculated. I expect my grandkids to go to college and am happy to contribute—although if it were entirely up to me, they'd only get assistance after taking a one-year break between high school and college to work in nose-to-nose, toes-to-toes direct selling, speak-to-sell, or both, entirely separated from the Internet and saving those earnings to invest in their own educations. My friend Nido Qubein—who taught himself how to speak-to-sell as an immigrant here, starting with a bare grasp of the English language and going on to become a top professional speaker, consultant, investor, corporate board member, and university president—graciously named me to the advisory board of the School of Communications at High Point University. Another good friend and great professional speaker, Dr. Herb True, taught at Notre Dame. I have no beef with you if you went to college or if you think doing so is important. I'd happily retire to a teaching post at a nice college with bucolic campus and mushy young minds to mold. But no college education can match street-selling education. And, very specifically, mastery of speaking-to-sell, which can only be accomplished by actually speaking-to-sell, can be a powerful springboard to many things, including wealth.

I do not know about me. Would I have wound up rich, relatively young, with great liberty, autonomy, and prominence, had I gone to college instead of going to work selling? I can't even hazard a guess. But I do *know for fact* just how valuable my education, featuring speaking-to-sell nearly from its start—begun with chalk, drawing circles—has proved to be. I can put a definitive price on it. And I can therefore highly recommend it.

If you are not yet speaking-to-sell, find opportunity to do it, work at getting good at it, and watch everything that happens because you do. If you are already speaking-to-sell, dedicate yourself to mastery and more and better use of it, and watch everything that happens because you do.

CHAPTER 2

The Man or Woman Who Can Speak-to-Sell Need Never Go Hungry

There are a lot of ways to make money—and *make an opportunity for yourself*—if you can speak-to-sell.

There is a pastor/televangelist I won't name, who has on several occasions proved entirely incapable of holding either a local mega-church or a TV ministry of his own together. He is a terrible businessperson, and he tends to get in trouble having sexual relations with parishioners and parishioners' wives and daughters and has been known to have a little gambling problem. But he can sell and guilt and shame and create hope from the pulpit like nobody's business. So he makes a *seven-figure* yearly income as an itinerant preacher brought in when a mega-church is running a major fundraising campaign for new buildings or TV studio or orphanage or whatever, to speak to raise that money. He is paid a percentage of the take. He is not alone in this, by the way; there are other itinerant pastors who go from church to church as guest speakers, who are paid via sharing in ticket receipts for special events, selling their own seminar after their sermon, camping out for a week doing counseling sessions sold by sermon, and/or sharing in funds raised for a specific purpose. This guy happens to be the number-one dog in this hunt, but there are quite a few other ones eating well via this work.

In the "get-rich industry"—with old reliables like real estate or the newest fad-opportunity of the moment, like web sites on Internet malls or making money on eBay or Facebook—"preview speakers," who camp in each town for a week and do the free afternoon and evening seminars in order to get people into paid weekend seminars, where they are then sold pricey packages, routinely make $250,000 to $2.5 million annually. Since I have moved this system into niche markets, there are many niche info-marketers who employ one or two such "road show speakers," with fewer dates, less work, and smaller audiences but still healthy six-figure incomes. And there are many other info-marketers who could be selling and acquiring new customers this way who don't. If you can speak-to-sell, you could find such a "partner" this week and be making at least $2,000 a week by the fourth week. Right now.

There is no shortage of businesses with things that can be sold via seminars, that aren't using this sales method, and have sufficient trans-action size and margin or customer value to pay a speaker hundreds to a thousand dollars or more per sale, or at least thousands per speech, so anybody who (a) can speak-to-sell and (b) knows how to market to fill seats can always get exclusive rights from such a business to run a sell-by-seminar operation for it, and bingo, that speaker has a business. He could contract with two or three noncompetitive entities and do seminars selling on behalf of them all during the same week in the same city. This can apply to consumer products—I've seen high-priced water purifiers, in-home spas, laser therapy devices, even kitchen-countertop juicers sold via public seminars. It can apply to professional services—a group of high-income financial advisors I work with all sell via seminar, and many others in their profession could but lack the speaking ability and confidence to get up there and sell, and a stand-in could do that for them. I and a chiropractor client of mine did the first public seminars selling chiropractic manipulation-under-anesthesia, and I once owned one-third of a very successful sales operation, selling Mace keychain chemical deterrents, with speakers doing "crime safety seminars" at companies' lunchrooms, real estate offices, etc.—in that business, our top saleswoman made $50,000 part time in one year, in the 1980s.

Then there is in-home speaking-to-sell. There are quite a few Tupperware agents who earn six-figure incomes doing in-home parties. But lots of things can be and are sold this way, including cosmetic surgery, financial services, cruise vacations, Las Vegas vacations, home improvements, college planning services, home and personal safety products, personal psychic readings, and countless other goods and services. My earliest business experience included Amway, and I crafted and delivered my own home party and taught other distributors to do the same. I still recall an evening, at age sixteen, when I made over $1,000 at one home party. If you did that twice a week *today*, you'd clear six figures for the year; if you sponsored a few people and ran them as a professional party-plan crew, you could top $250,000 a year. That and a fat hog will get you through the winter.

The Internet and its webinars and media like YouTube have reduced the number of speakers who sell roaming the countryside, as well as the number of these kinds of road-show, preview-seminar sales operations—but for no good reason. The approach still works just fine, and I have several clients currently making great sums of money with the exact same model I used in 1983, right down to the same hotels in many of the cities. Back then, I created this opportunity for a speaker and paid him over $300,000 a year for the next several years. If I had a speaker who could sell, we could replicate it today.

Way back when, I built my first "herd" by speaking-to-sell. I spoke at every sales meeting occurring in the Phoenix area for free, to sell tickets to my own weekend training seminar, held every six weeks. I filled my own preview evenings, conducted every Tuesday and Thursday nights, where I sold people into the same weekend training seminar. At that seminar, I sold people into what today we would call a coaching group. In 1977–1978, I ground out over $100,000 a year net. It wasn't elegant. It was a lot of work. But it worked. And, with minor tweaks, anybody could do it today and do fine.

To get a fast foothold as an expert advisor in just about any industry niche, someone adept at speaking-to-sell need only create and aggressively promote a free seminar the day or just the evening before that industry's trade association's annual convention, in the same city, so that everybody coming to that convention need only arrive a little early to attend the free seminar. I did this one year in front of the National Speakers Association Convention, when I was marketing my services to speakers. I showed Bill Glazer how to do it when he was a niche info-marketer to the menswear industry, with an event the evening before its big trade show.

One way or another, the person who can speak-to-sell and who will work for food need never go hungry.

This is important, somewhat beyond the scope of this book, because the only *real* security is your personal ability to produce. Everything else can be rendered valueless, and just about everything else is at one time or another. A highly developed, relatively rare skill for which there is use and demand at any time under any circumstances is a very useful thing to develop and possess. I have two, but even having one is better than 99% of people. Right now, as I write this, America has the worst workforce participation since the Great Depression, despite the fact that there are five million empty jobs. A lot of people are unemployed or underemployed or unable to create good opportunity for themselves because they have failed to develop a high-value skill for which there is use and demand at any time under any circumstances. Not because they couldn't, but because they *didn't*. You can avoid their mistake and the peril of it, starting today. Speaking-to-sell fits the bill, but if not it, identify some other high-value skill to master.

CHAPTER 3

Who Can, Should, And Does Speak-to-Sell?

P rofessional speakers should never let themselves be work-for-hire, fee-paid laborers earning only a day's pay, but failing to create equity via creation of customers who can be retained and developed and who provide reoccurring income directly from subscriptions, products, courses, coaching, etc. The comprehensive explanation of this is in a program specifically for professional or aspiring professional speakers: *Big Mouth, Big Money*, available at GKIC.com/store.

But virtually any local or national business owner or entrepreneur or professional in private practice can speak to groups and/or use other one-to-many presentation opportunities to promote their businesses. Financial advisors, CPAs, attorneys, chiropractors, cosmetic surgeons, dentists, and other health-care professionals commonly use speaking for promotion purposes but especially clever restaurant owners and chefs, flower shop or gardening center operators, retailers of any sort, home-service business owners, martial arts school owners, to name just a few, also use public speaking as well as public seminars and workshops and in-office/in-store classes and events for marketing purposes.

Authorship and speaking for these purposes go hand in hand, incidentally, and if you haven't read Adam Witty's book, *Book The*

Business, to which I co-authored, I recommend doing so. I would argue that there is no one, in any business, who is foreclosed from opportunities to promote and grow their business by getting the right book published and promoted and by speaking about it, as the author of *The Book on* _____. In one instance, I nearly doubled the pulling power of ads and mailings for a financial advisor's evening "workshops" (to get new clients) by repositioning them as "An Evening with the Author."

It is rather easy to get yourself booked to speak *free*. Most communities are rife with women's clubs, civic clubs, chambers of commerce, networking groups, schools, community colleges, and countless local associations, most of which have lots of breakfasts, luncheons, dinners, and meetings for which speakers with interesting topics are needed—and, generally, budgets are slim or nonexistent. Beyond that, with some creativity, you can plumb groups' lists and influence in other ways. For example, if you assemble a how-to workshop, people can be induced to pay to attend, and you can "package" it and take it to one or more groups, to be promoted as a "non-dues revenue" or fundraising opportunity for the group. You might go together with several noncompeting merchants or professionals to create an event each person speaks at, each person promotes to their lists, and everybody shares the cost of bringing in one outside, paid, "name" speaker. If you have an unusual or interesting business, you can offer show-n-tell, behind-the-scenes field trips to different business or civic groups. If you have a book (see chapter 5), you can promote book signings and lectures at bookstores. Both independent shops and Barnes & Noble locations are friendly to local authors.

One-to-many opportunities featuring yourself as speaker can be created for your own lists of customers/clients/patients and accumulated, unconverted leads plus their friends and families, off-site or small group, in your place of business. Using the free mini-seminar, workshop, or class on a specific product or service as a lead generator into your own lists can be a very productive strategy, especially in high-transaction businesses. For example, a dentist conducts an implant seminar, marketed only internally, to his lists, for his patients and family members. Doing this quarterly, the last I checked in with him he was averaging about fifteen people at each in-office seminar, held on a Thursday evening; immediately getting four to six cases booked, each worth no less than $6,000; $24,000 to $36,000 each seminar; $92,000 to $144,000 a year. The owner of a restaurant, bakery, and gourmet food shop holds party-planning workshops in April and May, in advance of the big summer party season in his area. He promotes only to his own list. In 2012, he booked over $200,000 in catering from these little workshops.

Most business owners never do enough interesting things for and with their own audiences—customers, past customers, leads, and friends and family of the customers and prospects. Two such things that can be done for these audiences are classes for them and offering the business owner as a speaker—to them as well as through them to the groups they belong to.

The thing that interests most business owners most, though, is "virgin" prospects, customers, clients, or patients, and there are countless opportunities to get 'em in large numbers in a hurry by speaking. As I mentioned, a strategy I've helped a number of my B2B clients use, and I've used, is the scheduling of a seminar the day before the industry's major convention or expo and promoting it— instead of or in addition to exhibiting at the exposition. In one case when I did this myself, I put nearly three hundred good prospects in an all-day seminar with myself as the featured speaker, the day before their industry convention. Exhibiting in a booth for the three days of the show, I could never have had meaningful discussions with three hundred prospects. Instead, I did not exhibit but used those three days for private, one-on-one appointments, created at my seminar, in my hotel suite, and I closed over $500,000 of business. At the consumer level, I worked with a group of sixty top financial advisors who promote their own public seminars, workshops, and "evening with the author" events with themselves as featured speakers and very efficiently attract, screen, and sort fifty to two hundred prospects at a time. Being able to can be an enormous competitive advantage, because you then *can* and *will* do what your competitors can't and won't. The manager of the Dunkin' Donuts is never, ever going to do in-store Halloween party-planning classes or go speak at community groups about "Baking Better"—but you, the owner of your own independent Main Street bakery, can. And if you do so as the author of the book *Is Baking Better Than Sex?* you'll draw crowds. (I once had a client who authored a book titled *Aphrodisiac Cooking*.)

CAN YOU SPEAK-TO-SELL FOR REALLY BIG BUCKS? OF COURSE YOU CAN.

The big, big, big money is in creating or obtaining something relatively pricey that you can sell by speaking for yourself or as a "hired gun" for someone else—making the sale in one step, while on stage, with no follow-up appointments or other labor and activity required. When selling my home study courses and business improvement packages, I routinely had $50,000 to $100,000 days with relatively small groups of business owners brought together by a company, association, or promoter. In, money in hand, done, out and gone, all in a matter of hours. There's a doctor I know, who is very successful marketing various cosmetic procedures done with a particular type of laser equipment. That equipment manufacturer has him speak about his marketing and, of course, their equipment at trade shows and conferences and at one-day "field trip" workshops held at his clinic once a month—and he has earned as much as $650,000 in one year from ten of the workshops plus about a dozen other engagements. He does nothing but speak-to-sell. The manufacturer promotes the presentations, assembles the audiences, and takes care of the buyers.

Opportunities to promote your present business or create an entirely new business or career by speaking-to-sell abound. If you have or create a "big-ticket item," you can sponsor yourself to speak.

Personally, I am often speaking for a fee *and* to sell some resource package immediately with the speech *and* feeding interested people to GKIC.com for membership *and* engaging in "whale hunting" for my own professional practice as a consultant and advertising copywriter. These are synergistic purposes. As an example, in 2015, I was hired by a client to be the chief guest speaker at his Sovereignty Summit, held in London, England, at Highclere Castle, the home of Downton Abbey. I was paid a fee to be there, plus first-class travel and lodging for my wife and I; I was promoted to his entire list even though only about sixty out of tens of thousands would wind up in the room—free advertising for my books; I sold resource packages to the audience; I whale-hunted and sparked two people into booking consulting days (at $19,400 each) and one into booking a copywriting and video script writing project ($100,000). In short, I got *five* kinds of compensation for the one gig. Just the whale-hunt opportunity would be sufficient. This is the kind of position you can put yourself in if you choose to master speaking-to-sell and you have a good business or businesses to feed by your speaking or will sign on to be used to promote someone else's business.

EVERYBODY HAS AT LEAST ONE *MARKETABLE* SPEECH IN THEM

Again, who can speak to sell and/or to promote their business? Anybody. Everybody. Most people have the fodder for more than one marketable speech. Frank Bettger was a former baseball player turned insurance salesman who struggled and then succeeded. He began giving a speech about how he went from struggle to success to local business groups, as a client prospecting exercise, and wrote a book, *How I Raised Myself from Failure to Success in Selling*, which became one of the all-time bestselling books about selling. And even if you have somehow managed to grow up, live, and do business with no story to tell, you can borrow someone else's story. My friend Joe Vitale was fascinated with P.T. Barnum, made a study of him, wrote a book—*There's a Customer Born Every Minute*—all about Barnum marketing principles, and has been booked numerous times to speak on the subject.

Sometimes a marketable speech *only* needs to be storytelling. I ghostwrote a speech for Joan Rivers' daughter Melissa, which she used countless times to promote her book about life with her mother, *The Book of Joan: Tales of Mirth, Mischief, and Manipulation*. Years back, a guy named Charlie Plumb got a lot of speaking engagements telling his story of survival as a P.O.W. in the Vietnam War. He and I were once seated next to each other at a lunch, at a convention where we were both speaking, and the plates plunked in front of us were full of rice with small hunks of chicken. He tasted it and ruefully said to me, "The rice was better in the prison camp."

The speech does not necessarily have to be directly linked to the business being promoted, particularly at the local level. The owner of the home and garden center can go speak about *Ten Secrets of Green-Thumb Gardening*, but he can also speak about *Growing Up Irish* and still be making his business known to audiences.

You *can* find a marketable speech to suit your business purposes.

CHAPTER 4

Speaking to "Manufacture" Authority

S peaking as a means of beefing up your authority positioning with customers or clients, investors, the media, or others is a proven and practical method.

Generally, more people are afraid of public speaking than of just about anything else. More men would agree to a date and a sleepover with Caitlyn Jenner than would accept an invitation to speak to an audience of a hundred. People vastly prefer *Snakes on a Plane* to an expectant audience waiting for wisdom or comedy to spew from their mouths. The entire Dale Carnegie empire was built on this fact. Ironically, the Internet's social media and abbreviated communication has made this more acute for those forty and younger; they are terrified and tongue-tied when asked to stand up in person and speak to a group of real people. The very fact that you will do it, and can step to the front of a room and do it capably and confidently, gifts you a certain level of authority. If you are put there at the front of the room by an organization, company, or host who already has authority with the audience, as he passes the microphone to you he also passes his or her organization's authority—this is the associative effect.

The person on stage, microphone in hand, starts with vested authority simply by being the person on stage, microphone in hand. From there, he builds on it or ruins it by his presentation.

But he starts in a good place. If a proper job has been done with that audience before he steps up there, so that background authority has been established and optimistic interest exists, he's even further along.

Overall, though, lasting, useable authority by speaking has to be re-useable and *repeatedly useable*. It has to be stuff you can show off, not just moments in time. This can include:

- statistics

- facts

- entity association

- celebrity association

- photos

- testimonials

- media credits

Speakers can pull together lots of statistics. Seventy-two% of the IBM executives who Joe Speaker did leadership training with rated it either "9" or "10" on a scale of 1 to 10. Seven out of ten real estate agents have attended Craig Proctor's seminars. More than half of the Fortune 500 have brought Sally Hogshead in to speak to their leaders about her book *Fascinate*. And so on.

Facts abound. If you travel a lot to speak, an illustration of a map with pins on it, every place you've spoken, can be a "Wow" item. If you've gone somewhere distant or exotic to speak, it makes you inter-esting. As mentioned, I spoke at a seminar at Highclere Castle, the home of the Downton Abbey television show, this year. I spoke two years in a row at the convention of the National Guild of Hypnotists. A training company I created had, in just three years' time, one-third of all the professionals in the market it served attend its seminars and hear its speakers. Speaking to a very large audience or a small but prestigious audience matters—I've addressed audiences as large as 35,000; I was once brought in to speak to the CEOs of six of the ten largest insurance companies in America. Speaking hands you facts.

Entity association offers authority. If you speak to "brand name" entities, highly respected entities, or, if local, locally known and respected entities, you have authority fodder. My friend Lee Milteer has, on her list of corporations that have hired her to speak to their troops, Disney, Federal Express, and NASA. That's gold. My friend Nido Qubein put me on the advisory board of the School of Communications at High Point University, and that is important to some people. Having a cache client can be extraordinarily useful, as has having Guthy-Renker as a thirty-year client been for me in the direct marketing universe. Giving a TED Talk can skyrocket authority.

Celebrity association is very powerful. Arguably, it shouldn't create authority, but it does. And, no offense intended, if you are as un-famous as one can get, you may, by speaking, wind up on programs that very famous people are also on—and even if you are speaking in a break-out session in the worst corner of the basement to twenty-two wanderers and the star is upstairs on the main stage dazzling 2,200, you still get to claim "appeared with," "shared the platform with," "appeared on the same program with." If you work in a niche, there may be niche celebrities you get to be on a program with. Of course, if you put on your own events, you can hire the celebrities you want to link yourself to as speakers. Among the many that we've had at GKIC events is Gene Simmons—so I joke that I've been an opening act for KISS. But joking aside, a lot of people think it's cool to have been on the same program with Gene and want to know about our backstage conversations. This is easy to make happen. You just need a check for the right amount that won't bounce.

Photos can establish authority. Photos with celebrities, experts, "name" clients, at meaningful places, with large audiences. It's best if these photos don't look awkwardly staged, as if with cardboard cutouts bought at Spencer Gifts instead of real people. In total, this is: we know him by the company he keeps. And it works.

Testimonials from audience members, clients, meeting planners, peers, colleagues, fellow speakers, and media figures can be extremely useful. I have testimonials from peers like Tom Hopkins and Brian Tracy that I have made a great deal of use of. We met and became friends by crossing paths as speakers. I have a great audience member testimonial that begins, "I jumped up and ran out of the room like a bat out of hell—because I had to act on Kennedy's amazing revealed secret immediately." Sometimes an academic testimonial can help, and I have a few from PhDs and, more useful with my crowd, I have this testimonial from the famous ad man Al Ries, the "father of modern 'positioning,'" beginning with his and Jack Trout's book, *Positioning: Battle for the Mind:*

> *"If you want to make waves, go to Harvard and get your Ph.D.*
>
> *If you want to make MONEY, get your Ph.E.—run to your nearest bookstore and get Kennedy's new book. It's a four year course in Entrepreneurship."*
>
> *—Al Ries*

Also this one from Somers White, once the youngest bank president in the United States:

> *"It was my good fortune to attend the Harvard Business School MBA Program. Most sophisticated business people agree it is the most highly respected school in the world. After graduating from HBS, if I had known then about Dan Kennedy, I would have immersed myself in everything he offered. I am bequeathing to my grandchildren the written materials, audios, and videos prepared by Dan Kennedy and collected and retained by me over the last twenty-five years."*

Media credits can be had by speaking, especially at the local level. If you are speaking about the sex lives of frogs or addressing the City Club about cyber crime in a small market and will do a little work, you can often get on a local TV show that same day or even get them to cover the speech live. Being on the CBS affiliate station in Wichita lets you stretch just a little and put the CBS logo into the montage of media credit logos you display at your web site. The huge seminar tour I was on was reported on by both *60 Minutes* and *20/20*, and although neither reported *on me*, I claimed and used the media credit.

Speaking can lead to *significant* media. The late Wayne Dyer wound up a star of PBS for years as a result of a book and speaking, and the book came from speaking in the first place. Larry Winget, author and speaker of "tough talk" business books, has appeared frequently on Fox Business Network programs.

Print media is sometimes easier to get and has longer-lasting value. The fact that you speak on a subject gives you a leg up on being accepted as an authority on that subject by a newspaper, magazine, or trade journal. In the 1980s, very soon after starting to speak a lot for chiropractic and dental groups, I was invited to write articles for and written about in a handful of those fields' magazines. One even named me "Practice Growth Guru Of The Year." These became long-used media credits. That positioning has lasted—as recently as late 2015, I was sought out for podcast appearances by the number-one industry media in dentistry. More recently, I was featured in an issue of *Success Magazine*, and that credit and reprint has extended-use value. I've reprinted that article here, at the end of this chapter. Long after I stop using it, the "As Seen In SUCCESS" will live on. I actually forget the year, years ago, one of my books was on *INC. Magazine's* 100 Best Business Books List, but the passage of time hasn't stopped me from using that credit or the broader "As Seen In INC." Were I to build a brochure, press kit, web site, etc. for myself today, I could and would use logos of *Inc., Success, Entrepreneur, Forbes, USA Today*, and *The Washington Post*, plus a dozen select industry journals, ABC, CBS, and so on as media credits, regardless of the fact that the coverage of me in those outlets spans and is scattered out over several decades.

The "action item" here is simple: examine any speaking opportunity you secure for every possible way you can extract from it or use it to create authority material. Think long, think hard, scheme, and work at it. As you build up your authority bank, you will see your actual bank account grow.

To that end, I need to mention the Authority Marketing Summit, which you can check out at advantageauthoritymarketing.com. I was privileged to be the featured speaker at the first Authority Marketing Summit. Its portfolio of ways to help people create build, and use authority is robust and growing, and there is no other organization totally focused on authority marketing.

SuCCESS

What *Achievers* Read

FREE CD *Inside:* Inspiring Talks with **Deepak Chopra, Dan Kennedy & More!**

START-UP
STRATEGIES
FROM
BUILD-A-BEAR,
FRESHII AND
PANDORA

3 TIPS FOR
WINNING
IN THE ONLINE
DEALS GAME

SCARLETT
JOHANSSON

"Doing what I
think I can't do
makes me
incredibly happy."

EXCLUSIVE
REPORT
AMERICA'S
HAPPIEST
(AND MOST
MISERABLE)
CITIES

CREATIVE
WAYS TO
RAISE
CAPITAL

5 TACTICS FOR
BECOMING A
SOUGHT-AFTER
EXPERT

20-PAGE BONUS SECTION

C'MON GET HAPPY!

○ 23 Easy ways to boost your mood
○ Why you'll be healthier and wealthier
○ How to reach your true potential

SUCCESS.com
June 2012

S Modern Marketing | DAN S. KENNEDY

Marketing by MAGNETIC Attraction

The principle of attraction is most frequently presented as a metaphysical concept, carried to foolish extremes—*thinking will make it so.* It won't, but it is a legitimate principle when applied in a practical manner, as in a marketing strategy, and that's what my trademarked Magnetic Marketing System is all about.

The idea is simple: Almost all marketing and prospecting is done as hunting, which makes potential customers or clients feel like prey. This naturally produces resistance. I prefer selling in a low-resistance environment, in which the consumer feels he is discovering, selecting and coming to you rather than your appearing uninvited and pushing a proposition. He has to choose you.

The smart questions are *not:* How can I "get past" the gatekeepers? How can I "get" an appointment? How can I "lure" a prospect to my showroom, store, preview seminar,

webinar? And the worst question of all is: How can I sell something to somebody today? These questions have a primitive foundation: the caveman contemplating how he can find and kill a beast today so he and his brood can eat tonight.

Instead here is the much smarter, more sophisticated question: *How can I set up a system of attraction that brings a steady, reliable stream of ideal potential customers or clients to me, asking for my advice or assistance as a trusted authority or provider in their category of interest or, even better, who are predetermined to be my customers or clients if accepted?*

This is a much more complex question. It represents a major shift in approach. If you can accomplish this for your business, it might beneficially (and maybe radically) alter your entire experience of doing business. This question's answers can eliminate commoditization

On CD.
Listen to Dan Kennedy's interview with Darren Hardy.

and make competition irrelevant, minimize price or fee resistance, facilitate price elasticity and higher profits, make your time infinitely more valuable, and create a less stressful selling scenario for you and your customers—leading to greater customer satisfaction and more referrals.

So let's be clear. Most advertising and marketing is product-centric and push-engineered: We've got this stuff to sell; how can we sell it? The diametrically opposite approach is customer-centric and attraction-engineered: Who are our ideal customers, and how can we attract and interest them? In abbreviated form, I'm going to show you how such a Magnetic Marketing System is built.

There are three parts to my Kennedy Marketing Triangle: message, market and media. One is no more or less important than the other; nor should they necessarily be in a 1-2-3 order.

Find the Best Target Market

Precision targeting to a select group of customer candidates is the secret of both financial/time efficiency and magnetic attraction. Simply, each person wants most what is clearly and specifically for him or her, not for anybody and everybody. I want to know: Is this for *me*? Why is this for *me*? And in every business, there is a specific high-probability prospect. A few examples…

A client of mine had a service, priced about $10,000, to sell to dentists nationwide. He was struggling, marketing to the entire profession. Examining his earliest buyers, I identified three facts:

1. They were all in outlying communities, not big cities nor rural areas.

2. They were all 55 and older.

3. Their reason for buying his service—which would help them start a sideline business, a weekend-operated dental assistant career school—was to accumulate more money for retirement than their practices would provide.

This information enabled us to reduce the size of the potential market by nearly a third, spending 100 percent of the available resources on only 66 percent of the dentists—thus more per high-probability prospects—and spending zero on low-probability prospects. We mailed initial information only to dentists 55 and older and only in certain geographic areas.

This information also led us to re-craft the message toward dentists 50 and older who worried they would lack the financial resources to retire as hoped. In addition, the message mentioned accumulation of up to $1 million in three to seven years outside the practice for on-time retirement,

Dan S. Kennedy is an entrepreneur, marketing strategist, consultant, copywriter and author of *The No B.S. Marketing Letter* and 22 business books, including *No B.S. Grassroots Marketing for Local Businesses* (with Jeff Slutsky), *No B.S. Price Strategy* (with Jason Marrs), and *No B.S. Wealth Attraction in the New Economy.*

achieving what I call Message-Market Match. The result: His publishing business went from losses to huge profits, with well over $1 million in income over the next 24 months.

Years back, someone who had used my Magnetic Marketing System came to me with the bad news that it wasn't working despite his having followed my models for his message and for the media. He owned a carpet cleaning company and had tried a direct-mail campaign to people living within a convenient radius of his offices. A drive through these neighborhoods at 5 p.m. easily revealed a problem: These neighborhoods were dominated by small, cheaply built houses on tiny lots bordered by chain-link fences; "beater" cars were parked in driveways. A subsequent phone survey revealed a high percentage of renters. They were unlikely prospects for his premium-priced, high-quality carpet cleaning services.

By relocating the same campaign to streets featuring nice homes with well-manicured lawns and late-model cars in the driveways—and being certain to mail only to homeowners, not "occupant"—I delivered a return on investment of $7 for every $1 spent on the marketing campaign.

As you can see, *who* you deliver a marketing message to can be at least as important as the message itself. This means you have to know as much as possible about your ideal customer.

Most marketers practice blind archery, wildly and randomly firing off as many arrows as they can, hoping a few hit *any* target. When you use fewer arrows precisely aimed at one carefully chosen target, you can cut the fat, waste and frustration out of your advertising and marketing.

Tap the Power of a Magnetic Message

You are fascinated with your thing—your gourmet pizza, your chiropractic care, your financial planning and products—but few share your fascination. Most people are most interested in themselves and their lives.

A majority of the previously mentioned dentists had little interest in a second business. In fact, it sounds odd and difficult, and requires sacrifice of time on the golf course or with family. But the 50-and-older dentists were very interested in a speedy solution to underfunded retirement.

Some homeowners buy furniture because they simply need a couch, and some get carpets cleaned only because they have filthy carpets. But most are interested in other things: having a more

Modern Marketing | DAN S. KENNEDY

contemporary-appearing, more stylishly furnished, more beautiful home that impresses friends, or a healthier home environment for their new baby.

One client who sells mattresses priced at $4,000 to $35,000 (versus the national average price of $600) is not selling mattresses. The company sells a good night's sleep, guaranteed, to chronic back pain sufferers or insomniacs or snorers with sleep apnea. So here are two rules:

Stop selling stuff. Most marketing messages are about product and price. Make yours about something more interesting to your target audience. And second:

Stop appearing as another salesman. Most people don't trust salespeople and don't trust themselves with salespeople, so anxiety and resistance rise even if they are interested in or seeking a given product or purpose.

The following are three key ingredients that make for a great marketing message.

1. Be unique. In this economy, there is little tolerance for ordinary. You must be unique. Gardner's Mattress uses Demonstration Strategy: The company installed its Dream Room, modeled after a luxurious hotel suite, where a potential customer enjoys a four-hour nap on the mattress prescribed. The closing rate is 100 percent. Yes, *100 percent*.

In my practice as a direct-response copywriter, I use Process Strategy: In an ocean of other writers, I never take assignments or discuss tasks with new clients. Instead I sell only one thing first: a day of diagnostic and prescriptive consulting, at a fee of $18,800, in which I uncover opportunity and build strategy and projects.

For its Proactiv acne treatment products, my client Guthy-Renker used Place Strategy. The company was the first to move this type of product from drugstore shelf to TV infomercial and built a business worth more than $800 million a year.

Tom Monaghan originally skyrocketed Domino's Pizza from tiny shop to global empire with Guarantee Strategy. He did not promise the "best-tasting" or even "good" pizza, but focused on delivery in 30 minutes or less. That factor was the prime interest of working moms arriving home to hungry families and of the nearby dorms of college kids who'd smoked funny cigarettes, urgently needed carbs and were in no condition to fetch them.

A group of seven-figure income advisers that I've been coaching use Message-Market Match: They focus exclusively on retirees interested in creating income for life from accumulated assets, and they position themselves as experts with authored books, local radio programs, infomercials, targeted TV ads and "Evening With Author" workshops.

2. Offer information instead of pushing product or service. The core of a magnetic marketing message is information of profound interest to your target audience. My client Ben Glass III, a Virginia lawyer, advertises and promotes a dozen different consumer guidebooks, each linked to its own website, including *Justice for the Bicyclist*, *The Motorcycle Accident Survival Guide* and *Robbery Without A Gun: Why Your Employer's Long-Term Disability Policy May Fail You*.

Financial adviser Isaac Wright is one of about 100 who follow a model devised by me and financial industry consultant Matt Zagula in promoting a consumer's guide to finding the right adviser and his book *How to Navigate Your Way to Secure Retirement: A Retiree's Guide to Removing Roadblocks and Hazards While Gaining Confidence and Peace of Mind*. My friend Joe Polish and I brought this approach to the mundane and oft-commoditized service of carpet cleaning, with free recorded messages to raise consumer awareness about allergens and germs in carpet that isn't regularly cleaned.

In any business, you can differentiate by marketing information instead of products/services.

3. Market yourself as the go-to person. I recently visited four competing booths at a home show, each selling generators. I made it clear to all four I wanted to buy. They all bungled it. They buried me in technical information. They defaulted to cheapest price. I wanted to find a guy to trust with making the right decisions for me. This is what most people want in most product and service categories.

In my book *No B.S. Marketing to the Affluent*, I present an Income and Influence Pyramid. Behind it, this fact: The higher a person's income, the more he is being paid for *who* he is (in the view of his target market), than for *what* he does or sells. This is why Diana Coutu of Diana's Gourmet Pizzeria invests in world travel to compete successfully in pizza chef competitions and writes cookbooks and health books: It makes her a more interesting and important *who*, enabling her to sell large pizzas at $20 to $30 versus competitors' $5 specials.

This is why a simple switch—from offering a "Free Workshop" to "An Evening With the Authors" in financial advisers'

As a Dean Martin fan, Dan Kennedy was a "predetermined buyer" of the late crooner's vintage Rolls-Royce.

ads—provided one client not only an increase in attendees but also improvement in their quality (average investable assets).

Right Message to Right Market via Right Media

Media provide ways we deliver magnetic-attraction-engineered messages. No medium is inherently better than another any more than a hammer is inherently superior or inferior to a surgical scalpel. Purpose makes one better than the other.

One key purpose is effectively communicating with your target prospects in the way they prefer and are most responsive to. That means setting aside your biases and preferences, peer pressure and superficial cost considerations in favor of simply what works best.

As an example, consider online vs. offline media. Many marketers have abandoned Yellow Pages for Google Places, yet certain target prospects—notably the 55-plus age consumer—still prefer referring to the Yellow Pages and go there first. Consequently, astute advertisers are staying put and even expanding their prominence in the Yellow Pages.

Or consider these facts about direct mail that will surprise many young businesspeople: The 2011 Epsilon Research Preference Study shows that, despite 66 percent growth in use of online social media, direct mail remains the No. 1 choice by consumers for receipt of information in many product categories, including health, travel and finance. Big shock: The 18-to-34 age group still prefers receiving information in these categories via mail. Twenty-six percent of consumers rank direct mail as more trustworthy than online media, and 50 percent report paying more attention to direct mail than email. Of all media, the *least* trusted is social media and blogs.

In business-to-business marketing, one of the most telling and ironic facts is that Google uses direct mail to sell its pay-per-click advertising.

The use of direct mail for marketing and sales purposes rose by 5.8 percent from 2010 to 2011.

For more from Dan Kennedy, visit success.com/ DanKennedy

The best media strategy is comprehensive, integrated and sequential. To be comprehensive, every medium that can be made to pay needs to be used—because diversity equals stability. Relying on too few media outlets, or on the cheapest, opens you to vulnerability. To be integrated, all types of media need to be used, and online and offline messages are fit together into an organized system for delivering magnetically attractive information. To be sequential, a prospect's contact information is captured and then a series of follow-up communications occurs.

The principle is: Don't yell out a product-price offer and hope some people come to buy it. Instead get interest and permission from prospects to communicate with them repeatedly and persistently.

Ultimate Goal: Predetermination

Wandering a Las Vegas auto museum, my wife and I came upon Dean Martin's 1986 Rolls-Royce Corniche Convertible. I already owned three classic cars and had no need or garage space for another. But I am a huge Martin fan. Minutes later, I bought the car. I did not comparison-shop other Rolls-Royces of the same vintage: I had no interest in any others. I was predetermined to buy that particular car. So now you understand predetermination.

Today in Orlando, huge numbers of luxury houses are on sale at bargain prices but if you are predetermined to live in Disney's ultra-luxury community, Golden Oak, you'll pay full retail and top dollar. From the seller's standpoint, predetermination makes competition irrelevant and supports price elasticity. This is the *ultimate* goal!

The purpose of all the strategies I've described here is to have new customers or clients coming to you, predetermined to do business *with you*, if they can and if you'll accept them. **S**

CHAPTER 5

Write a Book to Speak About

Often, the same basic material suits book and speech. My client and an author of Advantage Media Group, Ted Oakley, a wealth advisor principally to entrepreneurs selling their companies, has written several books for that audience including *$20 Million and Broke* and *Crazy Time*. This exact same material works fine for speeches (as well as online video, interviews, and "fireside chats"). Being the author of the books automatically makes him more appealing and marketable as a speaker on the same subjects.

AUTHOR = AUTHORITY, IN MANY PEOPLES' MINDS.

The book is also a means of securing media and publicity, locally or globally, and both that media exposure and the distribution of the book itself can bring speaking opportunities forward. My first two books, *The Ultimate Sales Letter* and *The Ultimate Marketing Plan*, first published in 1981 and 1983, respectively, and still available in updated editions, both brought "out of the blue" speaking invitations. Ones I recall include Ski-Doo, Honda, and the Golf Course Superintendents Association. I also recall an instance where an interview I did for a magazine about one of my books produced three speaking engagements. Your book or books are also the best self-marketing tools to promote yourself as a speaker. You might think that a video or audio of your speech would be, but neither of those tools or any other so directly equal authority or celebrity. Being a published book author continues to have *unique* power. Authors *do* get asked to come and speak about their book.

Those first two books, and all books since, were born from speech material or provided speech material. I have always worked a circular, closed loop: book to speech/seminar to book to speech/ seminar to book.

There are three basic categories of books: self-published, subsidy or pay-to-play published, and trade published. I have had and currently have books of all three kinds. Self-published means you write it, edit it, format it, get it printed as you wish, making it look and seem as much like a "real" book as possible. Bookstore distribution is nearly impossible, except for the local author locally on consignment, but today, everybody has access to Amazon distribution, and if your chief purpose for the book is direct distribution as a substitute for or adjunct to marketing materials, self-publishing can work just fine. If you need or want professional assistance with writing, editing, and production, and you want full retail distribution, then pay to play is the better choice, and Advantage is the leader in that field. If you are patient and persistent, have the right subject matter and promotional platform, you can be paid royalties by a "real" or trade publisher, and be assured of retail distribution. Again, I am in all three places with different books, done for different reasons at different times.

For example, my book *Unfinished Business: Autobiographical Essays* is published by Advantage, the publisher of this book, too. A trade publisher wouldn't want it—I'm not *that* famous. The flop rate with autobiographies of broadly famous folks like entertainers, athletes, politicians, and criminals is quite high. But this book is extremely useful for me as a fast way for clients and would-be clients to know me, find affinity with me, and bond with me, so I want it professionally published. It's not just a vanity project; it's a purposed business tool.

My entire series of No BS books,[1] though, is at Entrepreneur Press, the brother of *Entrepreneur Magazine*, and I've chosen them for that series because they pay me, because they have had good retail distribution, because the books get advertised heavily in their magazine and their .com media, and because there is cache in being published by them.

I also have self-published books, such as *The Ultimate Success Secret*. The book *The Ultimate Sales Letter*, published by a trade house, Adams Media, was first a self-published, spiral-bound manual, *How to Write Million Dollar Sales Letters*. There is also reverse migration: a trade-published book the publisher lets die, revived as self-published or with a pay-to-play house like Advantage.

Many professional speakers make themselves famous and marketable with self-promotion centered around a book. Zig Ziglar, originally with *See You at the Top*. Nobody knew Tom Peters until his book *In Search of Excellence*, but he then became a highly paid, popular business speaker in corporate environments. More recently, Jim Collins and the book *Good to Great* are a comparable example. To be clear and candid, this does not happen like the prince kissing Sleeping Beauty and "Poof!" everything is magically wonderful. Publishers are all pretty good at publishing, but hardly

1   You can see information about many of these books at NoBSBooks.com. All are available on Amazon.

any are really good at selling books. That falls to the author. So being published only provides a certain kind of opportunity—the ante to sit down at the table and be in the game. But, leveraged properly, a book or books can launch or greatly accelerate and enhance a professional speaking career.

For the *non*-pro, utilizing speaking, locally or globally, as a marketing media, a book is the perfect helper. It can get media and speaking opportunities that might otherwise be denied. Just as an example, I was once interviewed on the monthly call and audio CD put out by the real estate giant Keller-Williams to their top brokers and agents—as the author of a book. They would never let me in there otherwise; in fact, because they sell coaching, and the company I founded, GKIC, sells coaching, they view me as a competitor. But the book literally altered their thinking about me. One of my clients has written and published five different, impossibly dull technical books on different industrial engineering subjects, and because of them, he has become a columnist for one trade journal, gotten articles about his books in others, and gotten a number of speaking opportunities at trade shows and engineering conferences—all promoting the piece of equipment he manufactures and sells. But he would never get that media exposure or those speaking opportunities to talk about his machine—he is invited to come and talk about his books. Note: this is the owner of a manufacturing company, making a patented device, sold B2B, to engineers in various kinds of factories. Don't tell me *you* can't come up with a book of interest to (at least) your target clientele and get opportunities to go speak as an author about that book!

Even if it's a self-published book—the *Northeast Ohio Spring Gardening Book* by Dave Pearson, chief happiness officer of Pearson/Magellan Gardening Centers—it will work with local media, and it will grease the wheels for getting local area speaking opportunities. In Dave's case, it changes his position from "business owner promoting his business" to "expert and celebrity author." It also provides the subject for Dave's speech itself.

To shamelessly "plug" my friends at Advantage for a sec, the reasons Dave might better work with them than publish as a do-it-yourself project are: (1) they have any and every needed assistance and service under one roof, including "Talk Your Book" ghost-writing, editing, formatting, cover design, website for the book development, video for book promotion production, distribution, and publicity; (2) they have mastered the process, working with over 1,000 authors, many publishing for the same reasons Dave would; (3) time is money—Dave has a business to run, and Advantage offers a time-efficient approach; and (4) it will actually get done, rather than be a procrastinated-over, delayed project. But regardless of how Dave gets published, he definitely should publish. And if he wants to speak, that goes triple.

Great Books from Great Speeches

Dr. Maxwell Maltz delivered his "findings" about the self-image first as a lecture, before converting it to books—first, a clinical book intended for doctors, published as *New Faces, New Futures*, then, in 1960, the mainstream self-help book *Psycho-Cybernetics*, which has sold well over 30 million copies, created a new thought movement about self-image psychology, and, in his time, made Dr. Maltz a famous celebrity and a wealthy man. I never met Max, but I did meet and spend some time with his wife, Anne, while working on a TV infomercial project and subsequently acquiring all the rights to his works—then coauthoring a book, *The New Psycho-Cybernetics*, with the late Dr. Maltz, using it as basis for a bestselling audio program published by *Nightingale-Conant*, and creating a second book, *Zero Resistance Selling*. Ultimately, all rights and the business were sold to an information marketing entrepreneur, Matt Furey.

Dr. Norman Vincent Peale's mega-bestseller of the same era, *The Power of Positive Thinking*, evolved from Peale's church sermons. Of more contemporary timing, Pastor Rick Warren's mega-bestseller *The Purpose-Driven Life* has identical roots: sermons.

Zig Ziglar's book *See You at the Top*—which has sold over a million copies—is entirely constructed from his speech material. Quite common for speakers to convert speeches and seminars to books, even before they could put them out in audio media. That includes Charlie "Tremendous" Jones, J. Douglas Edwards, Jim Rohn, and countless others. One of the all-time best-selling books about selling, *How I Raised Myself from Failure to Success in Selling*, came from its author, Frank Bettger's telling of his story to fellow insurance agents at his company's conferences.

Dale Carnegie's book *How to Win Friends and Influence People* came from his classes about public speaking, and became the force that fueled the establishment of those classes as a popular national institution. For a time, it was nearly automatic: when a corporate executive got promoted, he was sent to the Dale Carnegie course. His book's success also spawned many imitators, successful in their own right—notably Les Giblin's *How to Have Confidence and Power in Dealing with People* and Paul Parker's *Tact and Skill in Dealing with People.*

Al Lowry's original get-rich-in-real-estate book, which birthed an entire industry, was essentially his preview seminar speech put on paper.

CHAPTER 6

My Secret Sauce

O ver the years, as a professional speaker appearing at many big and prestigious events, selling truckloads of goods, and successfully "whale hunting" for clients, I've been asked—usually privately—by other speakers as well as aspiring ones for my "secret sauce." Some have been somewhat puzzled by my success, given my deviance from both speaking industry norms and my disinterest in traditional "performance art" issues. Once, an aspiring speaker in an audience accosted me afterward, offering to critique and coach me. He had meticulously stick-counted the number of times I'd said "uh" and the number of times I'd put my hands in my pockets, and he was profoundly disturbed by the haste with which I showed and took down slides using a visualizer rather than using a much more professional PowerPoint presentation operated with a hand-clicker, freeing me to roam the stage. In conversation I determined he made about $50,000 a year at his job, and I'd just made twice that in two hours, so I suggested he go establish himself as a million-dollar-a-year speaker, come back with tax returns, and then we would talk.

No, money is not the only measure of the merit of a person's advice. But all the greats tend to deviate from the norms and utilize their own secret sauce as speakers or stand-up comics or even corporate leaders. Me, too. In this case, my critic did not realize that each of my uhs was "planted": deliberate, matched with physical gestures, with deliberate, choreographed purpose. He did not understand the automatic mind-numbing effect PowerPoint presentations have, so even if okay for teaching, they're a terrible tool for selling. On and on. He had ideas and opinions. I had a selling system that worked consistently at a very high level.

As near as I can tell, McDonalds' secret sauces don't contain many secrets. That stuff on the fish sandwich is ordinary, commercial tartar sauce plus a whole lot of sugar. The stuff on the Big Mac® is ordinary, commercial Thousand-Island salad dressing plus a whole lot of sugar. There's a theme there.

Warren Buffett has a secret sauce recipe for buying big into seemingly diverse companies. As I write, for example, he owns jewelry and furniture stores, NetJets, the Pampered Chef party-plan company, and railroads. It looks odd, just as my speaking sometimes seems odd to the uninformed, superficial observer or critic. But you can't sensibly criticize Warren Buffett; he's one of the ten most successful professional investors of this time or any of the past five decades. It is more useful to try and find the method to the apparent madness than to have "constructive criticism" for him or critical opinions about his choices. For the record, he's relatively transparent about the ingredients of his secret sauce, but that doesn't stop a lot of people from being blind, deaf, and dumb about it. Iger at Disney and Trump also have a secret sauce for acquiring and investing in things, and its secret ingredients are visible and openly talked about, but this never seems to end the recurring "experts" hollering about those guys grossly overpaying each time they make a major investment. It amuses me. I'm sure it amuses them. The oft-heard critiques of my speaking and my speeches has also given me a great deal of amusement and entertainment. Feel free, as Dino said, to keep those cards 'n letters coming.

For virtually all my speeches, I work with a much more complicated recipe than McDonalds' secret sauces but probably a little less complicated than Buffett's investing formula. In any case, there are key ingredients put together in a particular way, in calculated ratio to each other and with specific purpose. Here is almost a complete ingredients list—not in any order of priority.

Provoke 'em. That means picking fights, sometimes with government, political figures, public figures, industry leaders, famous authors, in much the same way Trump picks fights for self-promotion or, recently, as a presidential candidate. It means using the three subjects speakers are traditionally told to avoid—sex, politics, and religion. It sometimes even means picking on someone in the audience or even criticizing the entire audience. I want my audiences engaged, not passive.

Make 'em gasp. The reaction I want, at least several times through the speech, is; I can't believe he said *that!* I almost always want this at or very close to the start. The psychological term is "thought pattern interrupt." People are creatures of habits, including habits of thought. If you want to knock their mind's posted guards down and gain entry to present a new idea, to persuade of a different action, etc., you have to disrupt their habitual reaction to anything remotely resembling that idea.

Give 'em something to talk about, argue about amongst themselves, gossip about amongst themselves. I think the movies that get the best word-of-mouth boost are those that get people talking about points or ideas or situations raised—not just get people saying "that was a good movie." Movies that present moral dilemmas, seriously or in comic form; movies that suggest conspiracy theories; movies that have a profound point of view. A lot of talk I heard about the movie *Batman Begins*—by far, the best Batman movie, truest to the Dark Knight character—had to do with the ethical debate between Batman/Wayne and Alfred over Wayne's secret surveillance and eavesdropping on *every* phone conversation in the city, an obvious play on our own post-9/11 crisis panic, our Patriot Act. I want to do this. I want to give them something to talk about, debate, question, get into arguments over. Whenever I talk about productivity, for example, I emphasize extreme rigidity in scheduling, day-scripting, and control of access, knowing it produces discussion afterward—with people arguing about its impracticality, freakishness, interference with spontaneity or creativity, and so on. If you read any of my No BS series books—which are, essentially, speaking-to-sell in print[2]—you will find a staking out of dramatic, provocative, and controversial positions. I do not believe in vanilla. I am not interested in being unobjectionable.

Make 'em laugh. Refer to my book, *Make 'Em Laugh & Take Their Money.*

Present three key, memorable ideas. Most of my speeches have three memorable ideas—no more, no less, often triangulated. My "Multi-Million Dollar Speech" selling *Magnetic Marketing*®, for example, is divided into thirds, followed by summary; the thirds: message, market, media.

---

2   Books are just a type of media. Many books are written just to be books. Mine are conversational in style and tone, like speeches and like conversations—not literary or textbook in style, because they are speaking-to-sell in print, not writing to inform or instruct. With every medium, know and honor your purpose.

- message
  - unique selling proposition
    - offer or call to action
    - guarantee or risk reversal
- market
  - target marketing
    - demographic
    - psychographic (vs. simple geographic)
- media
  - direct mail
    - three-step sequence
    - endorsed mailing

Formula: 3 over 3, 3X. That's actually a lot delivered in a seventy-five to ninety-minute time frame, so careful organization is required, as well as great clarity about the objective—which, in this case, is *not* "understanding" but instead, enough understanding of three areas of relative ignorance and inadequacy and an opportunity to do something more sophisticated and productive, creating desire to buy these things in useable form. I strongly believe in the power of three, the power of triads.

By the way, most people seeking to speak for acceptance, acclaim, or applause or out of the double-sided coin of ego and fear of disapproval, pack way too much into a presentation under the mistaken presumption that overdelivering drives audience satisfaction, sort of like serving a piece of pie three times too big to eat might impress. In fact, consciously or subconsciously, they make impressing the audience and/or the host of the group their purpose. My purpose is getting money. Theirs: impressing people.

Name-drop. I want to connect myself to people they know of, admire, see as celebrities, view as credible authorities, are curious about, are interested in. I try to do most of my name-dropping in context of stories in which I star, rather than, say, just quoting the other person. Fortunately, I have a lot of these anecdotes, and I have actual association with a lot of celebrity entrepreneurs, celebrities, authors, and experts. I can tell a true story about my backstage conversations with Donald Trump or Gene Simmons of KISS, my work with Joan Rivers or name-brand companies like Weight Watchers International, or my infomercial work with the likes of Robert Wagner or Rose Marie from the original *Dick Van Dyke Show.* (If you can't, by the way, you can start making a point of such useful association, and you can at least pick a few "name" individuals to study and become an expert in, so that you can talk about that study and reveal little-known facts and stories and strategies about those people. I do not know Buffett, but I've made a serious study of him and can speak about him credibly and expertly. And my audiences know of Buffett.)

Tell signature story or other "big bang" close. A lot of speakers just trail off or end abruptly with the pitch itself. It is better, however briefly, to close the door on the speech in an emphatic manner. It can be as simple as a relevant quotation from a famous source. Or it can be a summarizing story, as in my *Magnetic Marketing®* speech. One way or another, your lasting impression is from the way you start and the way you end. Of course, when speaking-to-sell, you can't slow down the stampede, so you often have to awkwardly put this before the bridge to the pitch, but there should still be some small yet powerful thing that occurs within or at the end of the pitch.

Offend. I believe you resonate proportionate to willingness to offend, ideally done in a way to resonate with many at the expense of offending a few—although there are times when your speaking opportunity is, in fact, a fishing expedition when deliberately offending many to resonate with few is the required strategy. If you are intimidated and overly cautious so as not to offend anybody, you'll probably fail because there's always some idiot trying to be offended, and you'll definitely fail at creating extremely strong connection with anybody. Based on this, I knowingly and deliberately incorporate attacks and jabs, stories, humor lines, viewpoints, etc. that I'm confident will offend some in the audience, make some in the audience uncomfortable, and make some in the audience dislike me. I know some will "lock on" to that one thing and hear or remember nothing else, but I'm willing to trade that for the heightened response I want from the particular people I want it from. To use comedy analogies, I don't want to be Sam Kineson or Andrew Dice Clay, but I don't want to be a carefully sanitized, un-objectionable comedian, either—I want in-between, maybe like Ron White. If you go back, a Bob Hope comedy performance was like vanilla ice cream—safe for Hope, good for you, but not anything you'll be telling everybody about days later, other than maybe the fact that you were there. I need a stronger reaction than that. I am not trying to come and go without incident.[3] I am trying to draw out of an audience some people, often a relatively small number of people who find me absolutely fascinating,

---

3   At Glazer-Kennedy and GKIC SuperConferences℠, we got a smattering of complaints because Joan Rivers said "fuck" and viciously made fun of certain kinds of people. We got as many or more complaints about supermodel Kathy Ireland and Zig Ziglar giving personal Christian belief testimony. The only way to offend no one is by saying nothing, doing nothing, achieving nothing, and staying home.

magnetic, and irresistible. To achieve that, others, sometimes many, must find me objectionable and annoying, if not repulsive.

Here is as good a place as any to mention the power of what Dr. Maltz, author of the thirty-million copy bestselling classic *Psycho-Cybernetics*, and coauthor with me of *The New Psycho-Cybernetics*, called: **the power of immunity to criticism.** This is much more powerful than Dr. Peale's power of positive thinking. Most real "top performers" at anything including speaking and especially speaking-to-sell have very, very high immunity to criticism. Most failures are hypersensitive to criticism. Howard Stern took a caller offering feedback to school on this subject on his radio show one day in 2015, and I have placed a written transcript of that call at the end of this chapter. It's funnier if heard rather than read, but it is very instructive with gems throughout, so reading it carefully, several times, is called for. Most will, by habit of thought, and ingrained (yet erroneous) beliefs about how to be successful, react badly to this. You may be revolted. You may disagree. You may excuse yourself quickly, with "Well, that might be right for Stern the Shock Jock, but it can't be right for me." But peak success is peak success.

Appear to be having fun up there, and be playful. Audiences like to believe the speaker is enjoying himself and having a good time up there—*likes speaking and likes them.* They don't respond well to stiff, uncomfortable speakers who seem to telegraph that they'd rather be somewhere else. I can respond spontaneously to opportunities to be in-fun and playful with the audience—say, if they groan instead of laugh at a joke or somebody calls out something, but I also engineer several situations in that I know will create such opportunities. If they sense that a speaker is anxious or scared, bored and going through the motions, disconnected and delivering a slide show—they tune out or may even become visibly, audibly restless or hostile. "Old masters" like Jim Rohn and Zig Ziglar delivered entirely canned presentations as long as three hours in length that felt to the audience as if personalized for them and fascinating to Jim or Zig. Getting and watching video of a Jim Rohn presentation is worthwhile for this reason, as well as the content. Speaking strictly to sell imposes time constraints and usually requires a faster pace than Rohn's, but the feeling the audience gets is still the issue.

By and large, people respond well to anybody who seems to like doing his job, whatever it is, and seems to like the consumers of the job he's doing for them. Different people who drive airport shuttles and cabs, wait tables, tend bar, etc. in the same places get vastly different quantities and size of tips because of this simple truth. Customers tip more to the guy or gal who seems to be happy doing their job and happy to be doing it for them than they tip to somebody doing the same job who seems bored and listless about it, awkward at it, or outright disliking it. Same for a speaker. That is not license to deviate from script and just have fun up on stage. As Larry Winget says, it's called work for a reason. But you can be seen whistling while you work—or whining. This means, by the way, that you must be able to relax. The surest foundation for being relaxed as a speaker is to be delivering a purposed, organized, scripted, practiced presentation you know and are confident in and to use visuals like I use my paper-slides to ensure you are on track and on time.

Use lists. *The four keys, the seven steps, the nineteen elements*—lists like these are very useful for several reasons, so I have them in just about every speech. First, they work well as faux content; they are actually merely what-to-do lists, not how-to content, thus of little or no practical, actionable value (without also buying what I'm selling), yet they feel like they have weight and value—evidenced by how many people hastily try to write them down. Second, they can provide organization and structure for the speech. Third, they can be referenced when selling the product or service. Fourth, they can demonstrate that there is a lot of depth to what you do. Finally, you can skip a few items on the list, visibly, purportedly reluctantly, due to time pressure, thus leaving some curiosity aroused and entirely unsatisfied. In situations where you must give handout material, lists can meet that requirement without getting in the way of your selling work.

Confuse. A *little* confusion can be a very good thing. People with interest aroused, who see opportunity or benefit and value in what you present but who are somewhat confused about it and feel they aren't grasping it all are more easily motivated to buy it than are those who completely understand it. Most speakers believe the opposite to be true, especially those with an academic background or a lot of experience as trainers. Speaking-to-sell has its own best practices, including methods like this that may be counter-intuitive or contradictory to the experience of the speaker new to speaking-to-sell. Salespeople and advertising copywriters are even trained that "confused consumers do not buy," but that it is only true when in context with other truth, and in situations quite different from those encountered when speaking-to-sell. In my speeches, I want to introduce concepts and convince the audience of the value or benefit to be had by using those concepts, but I do not want them to think they fully understand the concept—instead I want them keenly interested in hearing more about it, learning about it, figuring out and being aided in figuring out how to use it personally. *I am after aroused interest, not complete understanding.* That last sentence is extremely important— please reread it. And make this mental note: even the best teachers make a lot less money than do the best sales professionals.

Also, I, and many of you, more need to create their confidence in us than to give them confidence in themselves. I need them to know I know what I'm doing. I do not, at this point, want them confident that they now know what to go and do. I want them to believe they can but also to realize they can't without me and whatever I'm selling. This is universal. The most effective pastor wants people to believe they can erase all the ills of their lives while here and even more importantly be welcomed past the pearly gates when they die—but he does not want them merrily strolling away thinking they can do that without him, without returning to church every Sunday and twice on Easter, without tithing.

Imprint what I want known via story. In most speaking situations, one of the things I want known is that I am available for private days of consulting (as I write this, at an $19,400 base fee) and available for direct-response copywriting projects, requiring substantial fees and royalties—but I am never actually speaking-to-sell these things and am almost always speaking to directly sell something else, usually a "hard" product. I am still also using the speech as fishing expedition, in case there is a whale[4] in that audience. Another thing

---

4   A "whale" is a very big fish—for me, the potential client with sufficient size and scope of opportunity and value from my expertise that he can justify project fees upward from $100,000 to $1 million. For the financial advisor, a whale might be the recent retiree with $500,000+ in investable assets sitting idle in bank CDs and IRAs. For the cosmetic dentist, a whale might be the divorcee, age 48 to 58, who got the house. Bill Harrison gave me a great book about Las Vegas' whales—about a top-dog casino "recruiter" and host, Steve Cyr—called *A Whale Hunt in the Desert*. If you can find a copy, it's a good read. Public speaking can be a very inefficient yet effective way of whale hunting. By ratio of whales to non-whales in an audience, it's usually inefficient—there may be only one per few hundred or thousand or even ten thousand. But if you are going to speak there anyway and sell something a large percentage of the audience can buy, you might as well throw out some bait for any whale that might be there as well. Just as an example, years ago, on a panel at the Direct Marketing Association, there to talk about infomercials, I worked in whale bait—mentioning my work with long-form copy direct mail, particularly with information and education products. And there was a whale in the room—the giant advertiser, International Correspondence Schools. I wound up banking six-figure fees from ICS.

I want known is that I prize autonomy above all else and can be "difficult"— or, as the little door-hanger on my conference room with a photo of a cactus says, "prickly"—when bothered. I want it known that I work dramatic, transformational magic in business by my complete marketing systems. There are usually about five things I want to make stick, known about me, and repeated about me to others. I will assert these, but I also try to imprint them via stories.

Imbed dog-whistle language. There is, for every group, unique tribal language that demonstrates my understanding of them; that I am not just delivering a canned, off-shelf speech. There is even more exclusive dog-whistle language that only certain people in the audience will hear and will go unnoticed by most. As example, there are specific philosophical terms that serious students of Ayn Rand recognize and, if hearing me say them, will recognize me as a kindred spirit—but that will have no resonance with anyone else. There are incidental disclosures—for example, that I stuttered as a child—that go unnoticed by all but someone who has or has had a speech imped- iment or has a son or daughter with a speech impediment. One of the things about speaking-to-sell that most people do not grasp is that it is not just broadcasting but is also about connecting with each individual in the audience, one at a time, one-to-one, multiplied. I call this "knock 'em down, one by one." For this reason, there is a lot of different dog-whistle language and a lot of varied incidental disclo- sures imbedded in my speeches, each of interest only to one or a few.

Throw 'em red meat. This is political terminology—a politician throwing red meat to an audience. The term means a "morsel" the particular audience will leap on like starving dogs and will absolutely love the speaker saying. In the 2008 campaign, it leaked that, while speaking to an ultra-left, liberal, elite audience at a fund-raiser in

San Francisco, Obama referred to heartland of America voters as "fearfully clinging to their guns and Bibles"—as means of labeling them as ignorant and as racists. For that audience, it was tasty red meat, thoroughly enjoyed and appreciated. Had he delivered the same line while speaking at a VFW Hall in a small town in Pennsylvania, Ohio, or West Virginia, they'd have clubbed him to death with their Bibles, then riddled him with bullets from their guns. In the early days of the 2012 campaign, Trump threw red meat to ultra-right, conservative, Obama-hater audiences by jumping to the front of the parade of people questioning the authenticity of Obama's birth certificate, his birthplace, and thus the very legitimacy of his presidency. Jerry Seinfeld promptly canceled an appearance at a Trump event for charity, and a group of liberal INDYCAR fans—their existence a surprise to me—launched a petition drive to oust Trump from driving the Indy 500 pace car in 2011. Those experiences did not, obviously, deter Trump from similar oratorical fire-bombing in his 2015 campaign.

Red meat to one audience is poison to another. It can carry a heavy price if your throwing it to the right audience is widely revealed outside that room, and in this day and age, the cellphone video camera and YouTube make that easy and even likely. So this tactic ought not be used casually. But I do almost always use it.

Present a philosophical core. I have long believed that there should be something of significance that I'm *about*, that I stand for, that I champion, and that I should reinforce it within every speech and at every opportunity. For the aforementioned Kathy Ireland and Zig Ziglar, for George Foreman, and for the promoter of the giant SUCCESS events that I appeared on some two hundred times, that "something" is their Christian faith. For people like my friend Robert

Ringer, author of the mega-bestseller *Winning Through Intimidation* (updated as: *To Be or Not to Be Intimidated*), it is a libertarian political viewpoint. For my friends, both no longer with us, Jim Rohn and Charlie "Tremendous" Jones, it was serious studentship. For me, there are several, but probably most important is self-reliance and personal responsibility (as key to unlimited possibilities). Even in the most "technical" of speeches about how to do a specific thing, I tend to work to my philosophical core, and as I've gotten older, more experienced, and more able to dictate what speeches I'll give, I choose subject matter conducive to conveying that philosophical position.

This contradicts the safe 'n vanilla idea, which is the most common advice given speakers. So, by habit of thought, again, you may find it hard to embrace. Many think they must hide their philosophical core. More often than not, doing so is more harmful than helpful, and it is definitely more stressful. My own practice has been extreme transparency about self.

" 'I yam what I yam an' tha's all I yam!' What the hell kind of résumé is that?"

Let 'em identify with me as a flawed human being. Getting up on stage and lecturing people about what they should think, how they should behave, or how they should operate their businesses is a declaration of superiority, that, if perceived as unmitigated egotism and arrogance, is likely to be resented by many and get in the way of selling. Still, selling is an act of intimidation or at least of prescription, requiring acceptance as someone superior and thus qualified to tell them what they should do. Without that, mass obedience to marching orders can't be achieved. Within that context, I think it important that I let them see that I am "an imperfect god." A god, yes, but one imperfect just enough, in endearing and amusing or simpatico ways, that I am not resented or rejected as a practical role model. The story of my obliviousness to my house being on fire, and my identifying myself as foolish and stubborn in that story, serves this purpose. My references to my cluelessness about women, wife, and marriage serves this purpose.

Let me again use Trump and the 2015 presidential campaign, as I write this, shocking pundits and competitors with its longevity. The reason that Romney was resented and beaten like a bad dog about being rich is that he was apologetic about it and seemed elitist about it. Trump has no trouble from it, particularly with blue-collar folks— the kind who were "Reagan Democrats." First, he's not apologetic. But second, he is seen by the cabdriver or dockworker as one of them. How can *that* be? Because Trump is rich in much the same way they'd act if they hit the lottery. They'd get a big, gaudy, gold-coated, diamond-encrusted car, plane, boat, and house, trade in the old, plain wife for a younger, hotter, exotic one, and brag, brag, brag. And Trump is obviously flawed: the hair, the failed marriages, twice nearly bankrupt, criticized, lets slip profanity, and offends people— just like the cabdriver and the dockworker.

I have not made Trump's money, and there's zero risk of me ever occupying the White House,[5] but I've gone a long, long way, with a core audience of "lifers" who've first met me by my speaking and chosen to hang around and support me for decades because of this exact same approach.

Present self as mysterious. No one is really very interested in entirely, perfectly normal and ordinary individuals. There is, of course, no such thing. "Normal" really doesn't exist at all. Actor Jack Nicholson once said, on having his behavior questioned, that for every normal studio exec, producer, or actor you could find in Hollywood, he could name ten who paid hookers and aspiring actresses acting as hookers to pee on them. Most people keep these kinds of "abnormal" quirks private, thus there's a lot more seeming normalcy than real normalcy. Regardless, there are very few books, films, TV shows made about ordinary people doing ordinary things. The much-repeated myth about *Seinfeld* was that it was a show about nothing—but, like most ensemble cast sitcoms, even old, benign ones like *The Andy Griffith Show*—its pond was stocked with odd characters full of unusual behavior. As I realized that there were things about me and my behavior that people found mysterious, I deliberately emphasized and embellished those things in my speeches (and in my written works). In my case, not at all by accident, people are mystified by and very curious about how I get so much done; why and how I persist in not using cellphone, Internet, email; that I drive professionally in harness races; that I read so much and how I can read so much; etc.

Present self as heroic. Superman is the most famous and enduring of all comic-book heroes, an alien come to earth more than sixty years

5   If nominated, I will not run. If elected as president, I will not serve. If made king, I'll consider it.

ago and popular ever since, the subject of countless comic books, newspaper comic strips, full-length novels, cartoons, movie serials, movies, and TV programs. In all of this, there has never been a comic book, book, TV show, or movie about Superman's alter ego, the meek and mild-mannered reporter Clark Kent by himself, never morphing into the superhero with the fantastical powers. Who would be interested in Clark Kent as Clark Kent? Who would be interested in *any* Clark Kent as a Clark Kent?

You do not need x-ray vision or superhuman intellect to divine the secret to power and influence and celebrity. In my speeches, in individual anecdotes, and by overarching story line, I always cast myself as a heroic figure with *superhuman* abilities. For my introductions, I have superhero-ish, cartoon-character monikers like "The Millionaire-Maker" and "The Professor of Harsh Reality," and identifying descriptions like "America's highest paid direct-response copywriter." In my speeches, I have stories of the Fortune 500 CEO realizing he was paying me more per hour than he was paying himself—and me telling him why (because of my "super power"); of the client flying a planeload of executives to meet with me because I refuse to travel to consult—because I can (a "super power"); of my marketing strategies turning dust into gold, tiny enterprises into billion-dollar companies, broke failures living in relatives' basements or selling their blood to get money to buy my course while sleeping in their car turned into millionaire entrepreneurs. All this is my substitute for being faster than a speeding bullet, stronger than a locomotive, able to leap tall buildings in a single bound.[6]

Get points for candor. I am known for "No BS." That's my positioning, my brand, my appeal, my style. In every speech, overall, and in

6   For more about this, I urge getting an audio program of mine, *Personality in Copy (Customers for Life)*, available from GKIC.com/store.

some pointed way, I take the role of Truth-Teller.[7] When I speak about wealth attraction, for example, I discount the immensely popular video *The Secret* as simplistic and juvenile, in positing that "thinking alone makes it so," and I proceed to state inconvenient truths about why money moves from one person or place to another. I go out of my way to be blunt, even coarse, to emphasize that I am to be trusted to tell it like I see it, consequences be damned. Quite a while back, I was impressed by remarks made by Mike Vance, a former associate of Walt Disney's, about peoples' deep-seated yearning for and attraction to authenticity. I determined that this was something I wanted to be known for and have reputation for.

Reinforce brand/positioning. I just described one way I have of doing this—and the No BS brand built of my positioning has been very good to me and became very valuable. The newsletters built with it, which became the foundation of Glazer-Kennedy Insider's Circle, enabled that company to grow and expand and develop market identity so valuable, in 2011 a major private equity fund in partnership with a management team with track record of success in training industry stepped in and bought the company for a multi-million-dollar sum I can't disclose. Entrepreneur Media, publisher of *Entrepreneur Magazine*, also publishes the No BS book series, now numbering fourteen, over eleven years, with total sales globally in the hundreds of thousands of copies, to an intentionally targeted audience. The brand also graces logo apparel, has been licensed to certain niche-industry publishers, and attached to local networking groups and coaching groups in cities throughout the United States

---

7   Note: Pick and define your role(s). You are your own casting director. Two of my chosen, chief roles have been, as noted, The No BS Truth-Teller (in a world of gypsies, tramps, thieves, fools, and liars); and The Stern But Loving Parent. For MUCH more about this, get information from Adam Witty at ADVANTAGE about recordings from my presentations at the first Authority Marketing Summit. (http://advantageauthoritymarketing.com/)

and abroad. This brand *exists because of* my speeches and my development and reinforcement of it when speaking. I think every speaker needs to think about brand building (as bonus by-product of speaking-to-sell) and about brand reinforcement each and every time they speak.

Divide and conquer. This has two applications. Within an audience, there are some folks I'll win over, others I won't. This has as much or more to do with them as me. I try to decide in advance how those two groups divide, so that I can play to the ones I can win, by setting up self-identifying choices they'll make. By a series of these choices, they separate themselves into "winners" and "losers." The last choice presented, engineered to feel like the others already made, is, of course, buying or not buying what I'm selling.

Flatter 'em. I find some reason to praise the audience, appeal to their egos, and let them feel superior or special, usually early in the speech. All late-night hosts, from Paar to Carson to Leno and others sometimes sense a difficult, potentially unresponsive crowd, and they then start by telling them how bad, dumb, not-with-it last night's audience was, how much better they look, and how much more excited they seem. This obligates and manipulates the audience into being responsive, laughing wildly at every joke. It *is* a cheap manipulation for which I feel not a smidgen of shame. I also incorporate flattery into the actual presentation of whatever I'm selling, often acknowledging it's not for everybody but only for very serious students of great ambition; not for everybody—only for people who, then referring to virtues I previously identified in my speech. This makes purchase an act of validation of superiority and gives instant ego gratification, more akin to getting behind the wheel of the shiny luxury car, than the dull-by-comparison experience of investing in a home study course.

Inspire and motivate 'em. Buying most things involves hope and optimism, often contrary to prior disappointments with prior purchases of similar things. And not only aren't people independently optimistic about the purchase of a thing, they are not independently optimistic about themselves, either. They know they are procrastinators, quitters, poorly disciplined, often unable to follow instructions and plans, intellectually lazy, etc. Their garages, storage sheds, closets, and bookshelves are full of things bought and never or very briefly used. All this needs to be set aside in favor of new hope and new optimism. So, although I've long cringed at being called a "motivational speaker," in the most accurate sense, that is, in fact, what I am. As a result, I rely very, very heavily on "if I can do it, you can too" and "if they can do it, you can too" stories and inspiring "up against tough odds," "in defiance of disbelievers and critics," and "from the outhouse to the penthouse" stories of both famous and unknown persons. I usually present testimonials specific to my products as inspiring human-interest stories of one of the four types I just named.

The Big Promise. Religions all revolve around a really, really, really Big Promise. Everlasting life free of pain, filled with bliss, with God in heaven. Or that twenty-seven virgins waiting for you in heaven thing. I don't know how they landed on the number twenty-seven. None of us can match these. But I try getting close. The speeches created to sell my *Renegade Millionaire System®* offer the Big Promise of Autonomy. As I define it, it is a utopian "place," possession of god-like powers, liberation from all pain and suffering and frustration, here on earth. The speeches created to sell my *Magnetic*

Marketing System® told salespeople they would be forever freed from their hell on earth: "cold" prospecting. One of the great golden-age ad men, David Ogilvy, posited that the heart 'n soul of an ad is its Big Promise. In speaking-to-sell, you are a walking, talking direct-response ad, so your heart and soul should also be a very Big Promise.

"Anchors." You more easily make the new acceptable by anchoring it to the familiar or old. With audiences of certain age, I use a lot of nostalgic anchors. For any audience, timely references to current events are helpful, by connecting with what is immediately familiar because they've been watching it on TV and talking about it over coffee. Very familiar and generally well-liked businesses work well, so I often use Disney and Starbucks as examples.

Make their enemy mine. Every group has an enemy: it may be Washington politicians and high taxes. It may be "the suits" at the home office, clueless about what goes on out in the field, getting foot massages from concubines while the guys who do the real work—well, you get the idea. It may be the big-box store discounters, if talking to independent retailers. It may be the injustice of aging in a youth-obsessed culture, if speaking to fifty- to sixty-year-old women. Every group has an enemy. And there is the cliché: *if my enemy is your enemy, you are my friend.* This has not worked all that well as a long-term geopolitical strategy for the United States—for example, we funded Osama Bin Laden's war against the invading Russians in Afghanistan. He didn't stay our friend for very long and later caused the 9/11 attacks. And later, we killed him. But I'm not talking about long-term strategy; I'm taking about sixty minutes. And it doesn't matter whether or not there's much validity to the premise—it is how most people feel and instinctively react: if your enemy is their enemy, you are their friend. It's a quick shortcut to trust.

The CTA. That's the call to action. When you speak-to-sell, you always have a specific call to action, which I've talked about elsewhere in this book. If you do not have a CTA, do not delude yourself: you *aren't* speaking-to-sell. You're doing something else, whatever that might be, but you are *not* speaking-to-sell. As Zig put it, you might be a professional *visitor*, but you are not a professional *salesman*.

Visuals. I don't use PowerPoints, but I usually use an Elmo or Visualizer, so I will occasionally use a photo or cartoon. Sometimes I'll use objects. Sometimes little snippets of video. I often show personal things from my own life, like photos of my classic cars or racehorses. In a way, a speech is a TV program they are watching live. It helps to do more than standing, gyrating, and speaking. Sinatra famously said, "Any singer who needs more than a spotlight and microphone is a putz." But that was Sinatra. I've seen a few speakers who are just that and need no more, for minutes, hours, or even days. But most can benefit from some help.

Leave 'em wanting more. Pretty much whatever you're selling by speaking—goods or services or even diagnostic process appointment to then sell goods or services—involves more of you: you personally or your expertise or your products, services, place of business, or other connection. So a desire for more of you is important.

My list should not necessarily be your list, but if you're serious about speaking-to-sell, you will have a list like this, and you'll use it as you prepare each speech and check each speech against it to be sure you leave nothing out that can further the sale or put something in that can harm it. You'll use it to plan and choreograph your performance and behavior. You'll run you and your speech preparation and your speaking by your checklist like a pilot or astronaut runs his plane or rocket ship by checklist.

There are thirty items here, and, as I said, the list is not complete. There are a few more items I decided not to discuss. This should suggest to you that writing and preparing a speech that sells is a complicated matter requiring sophisticated thinking and thorough preparation. Frankly, I know there are people who get away with just slapping something together with nowhere near this much strategy behind it, getting up in front of an inordinately receptive group, and slaying them. However, when you do this for a living as I did for nearly forty years and earn a seven-figure yearly income doing it, or if optimum results matter to you enormously, then you'll want to give yourself every advantage, and that can only come from sophisticated thinking and thorough preparation.

Howard Stern Radio Show Excerpt

Okay, Evan go ahead. You're on in Burlington, Vermont, all the way up there in Burlington, my friend.

Evan: Hey Howard, how's it going?

Howard: Hey now Evan.

Evan: Now, listen, when I initially got on the phone, I was more fired up than I am now, but I want to give a constructive criticism to the show.

Howard: Not necessary.

Evan: What's that?

Howard: Not necessary.

Evan: No, no, but it is, you need feedback from—

Howard: No, I don't. I don't need any feedback. I come in here, and I do what I want. What do I need your feedback for?

Evan: Because that's how you figure out—

Howard: No. I figure out what to do by me. I am in charge of me, and I am in charge of the show. I don't need feedback. What do I need feedback for?

Evan: Well because I've always thought about it as like a community—

Howard: No, if I thought about the show as a community I'd be doomed. Your feedback is irrelevant. Your feedback is irrelevant.

Evan: How dare you!

Howard: What? I'm telling you my process, Evan.

Evan: I know, but I figured that I could maybe—

Howard: Your feedback is irrelevant. Whatever your feedback is, it is irrelevant.

Evan: I'm a paying customer.

Howard: I don't care, then quit. I don't care.

Evan: No, you can't do that. If everybody just quit—

Howard: Evan, Evan, I *can* do it. I'm telling you your feedback is irrelevant. Through my entire career I didn't ask people their opinion of my show. I don't *care* what you think. I care what *I* think.

Evan: That's very hurtful.

Howard: It is hurtful, but you know what?

Moderator: But weren't you going to say something hurtful?

Evan: Well no, see that's the thing—

Howard: No. His is *relevant*. His feedback is *relevant*.

Evan: Then I decided not to be because frankly Howard didn't talk about—

Howard: Evan, if I listened to feedback, I'd have quit on day one. Everyone in my career gave me feedback that I was horrible, but I ignored it.

Evan: That can't be.

Howard: What?

Evan: That just can't be, I mean people must have supported you.

Howard: No, no, no, no, no, no, no. My own *father* told me I was bad. If I listened to him . . . I don't listen to feedback. Feedback is irrelevant. The way that I was an innovator was to *ignore* the feedback.

Evan: No, but not of the *common* man, of the higher up—

Howard: The *common* man, there's no such thing as the common man. Are you *common*, Evan?

Evan: Well, I'm anything.

Howard: All right, well, when the common man calls I'll listen to him.

Evan: All right.

Howard: All right, now what's your feedback? Let's hear it.

Evan: Well, okay, here's my feedback...you... you... initially...

Howard: You know who listens to feedback? Elvis Durant. Go call him.

Evan: I don't know who that is.

Howard: He's a morning guy, Z100. He'll listen to you. They probably do all kinds of research.

Evan: No, no. Well okay . . .

Howard: Ryan Seacrest probably listens to feedback. He worries about what people think of him. I don't worry about what you think of me.

Evan: Why not?

Howard: Because you're *irrelevant*.

Evan: Of course you do.

Howard: No, I don't. I don't care.

Evan: You want to have a show that everybody loves—

Howard: If I have to listen to. . . A show that everyone loves is hardly my show. Most people don't like my show.

Evan: Howard, I've been listening—

Howard: Call Jay Leno, he cares what you think.

Evan: Jay Leno wouldn't ever pick up on a phone call.

Howard: Jay Leno calls people and says, "Did I offend you? I'm so sorry." He actually *calls* people, he worries about offending them.

Evan: See, I think when you hear my criticism, you're going to appreciate it.

Howard: It's irrelevant, but if you want to waste your time, go ahead.

Evan: Okay, well, so one thing like that I've learned from you is like the value of like psychology, like...

Howard: I gotta go Evan, you're boring me...

Evan: You're boring *me*.

Howard: All right, well then there you go.

Evan: All right, *fuck you, Howard.*

Howard: All right, fuck you too. I mean, if you'd get to the point. His feedback. What has he created? If I listened to him and every other asshole on the planet I won't have a show, I'll be backed up. That's how I got to where I am, listening to guys like him. Your feedback is *irrelevant*. Either I've got the gene or the ability to know what to talk about or not.

CHAPTER 7

Power of Purpose

Clouded, confused, foggy thinking

begets the same sort of results.

I first learned about the power of clarity and clarity of purpose from Paul J. Meyer, the founder of Success Motivation Institute. What he said on this subject made so much sense to me that I embraced it as one of my foundational, lifelong principles for success: *if you aren't getting the results you'd like or need from any activity, situation, or relationship, it's probably because your goals are not clearly enough defined, to yourself and to others.* In ensuing years, it became clear to me that most speakers were not crystal clear about why they were speaking. They went with a muddled mess of vague and often conflicting purposes. It's also common for me to begin a consulting day with new clients in a variety of businesses and discover they are also unclear about why they are doing what they're doing in advertising, marketing, and operating the business, and unclear about their personal purpose for going to the office in the morning.

Too many overlapping or, often, conflicting purposes castrate them all.

Every success is a complex matter, but every success also has *a* clear focal point, *the* determinate of success or failure. Most of us have multiple reasons for doing whatever we do for work or play or charity because we are complex creatures. But successful people also sally forth to each activity with *a* clear focal point, *the* determinant of success or failure. This is a key differentiator between exceptionally productive achievers and the rest of the world. On any given Saturday, thousands of people will go to the big shopping mall in your area, wander around, de-stress from the week behind them, be entertained, maybe meet up with a friend and enjoy a lunch, and so on. The high achiever in their midst will also do all those things, but he will have chosen to go to the mall to get a new pair of stylish, cordovan, comfortable shoes, and he will *not* return home without them. Many others might have had a vague hope of finding a pair of shoes that struck their fancy. He went with a clear picture in his mind of the shoes he intended to find, by doing so he magnetically attracted them to him and himself to them, and he knew instantly when he saw them that they were, in fact, the shoes he went to get. Very few people operate with such clear purpose in everything they do, but, then, very few people get what they want out of their careers, other activities, relationships—or trips to the mall.

SO WHY SPEAK TO A GROUP?

You might randomly think of a muddled mess of reasons: status or sense of it—a meal for your ego; that you feel you have something important or interesting to share with the world; that you seem to have a talent for it; to make yourself famous; to promote yourself, a business, a scheme, a cause; to prospect for clients; and on and on and on. And these can all be good reasons to go. But too many overlapping or conflicting purposes castrate them all. Clouded, confused, foggy thinking about why you're there begets similar results. And if you're unclear about your purpose, I can promise you that the audience will be unclear about its response. Besides, choices about which groups you speak to and which you don't, where, when, what speech you give, what's in it and what's left out, and how it is structured all depend on clarity of purpose. Success is best reverse engineered from a focal purpose.

Mark Twain said that anybody who would write but for money is a blockhead. I share his disinterest in uncompensated work, so I felt the very same way about speaking from the very beginning. I came to it for one reason and one reason only: to make money. It was quickly evident that selling things to audiences by speaking paid infinitely better than speaking for fees. The result: some thirty-plus inglorious years as a "platform sales speaker." I have *personally* sold well over $150 million of products and services via giving speeches and conducting seminars. I got so good at it I have also been very well paid to create presentations for other speakers and coach speakers in platform selling and have created quite a few "killers." You may or may not have such aspiration, but you almost certainly do have opportunity to stand up in front of some groups—others or those of your own making—and sell yourself, your business, your products or services. I have written this book for you, the occasional opportunist, as well as for the pro speaker. It is about one thing and one thing only, with no apologies: *how to separate an audience from their money and—ideally—have them like it.*

That objective, incidentally, is unabashedly shared by the leaders of some of America's most successful and best-loved companies, like Disney and Starbucks; places, like Las Vegas; and you should not permit yourself to feel uncomfortable about it. There is absolutely no legitimate reason to feel uncomfortable in any way about getting out of bed in the morning to be as highly compensated for whatever you do that day as is possible. People who do so make it possible for everybody to have a decent place to live. This is a belief system issue far more involved than this book can handle, but it is integral to it. As a starting point, I recommend my own book, *No BS Guide to Wealth Attraction in the New Economy,* as well as Stuart Wilde's book *The Trick to Money Is Having Some,* Dr. Maria Nemeth's *Energy of Money,* and John Tammy's book *Popular Economics.* This is a reading list to get you right with money.

How you feel about money and how you feel about getting it as your chief, focal purpose has a great deal to do with whether you get any and with how much you get.

My favorite scene in the HBO series *Deadwood* has one bar/gambling house proprietor telling the other that he wished they could just whack the customers over the head, drag them out into the desert, empty their pockets, and leave them there—it would be so much simpler than teaching them, dumb as they were, how to gamble and lose money. But, one says, *that* would be wrong. We want to provide value, during the speech—although as a practical matter that is, by time constraint, limited, and can fully occur only after the speech sells whatever it is selling. But while doing that, we also want to empty their pockets. If you are not clear, comfortable, and purposed about that, you cannot be successful at speaking-to-sell. This is at least as much about what Napoleon Hill called "definiteness of purpose" and "burning desire" as it is skill. Probably more.

Personally, just as Glenn W. Turner outright told his audiences, "if I could, I would just reach into your jackets and purses and take your wallets and your money—and force what I'm selling on every one of you," I believe enough in what I'm doing to feel just fine doing so. I am aware enough of their flaws when it comes to making good decisions and acting on them without hesitation to feel justified in forcing their decision making. So I don't think that whacking them over the head and taking the dough would be wrong. But it's impractical. My purpose in being there, though, is to come as close as I can to doing so. Your purpose should be the same.

Why am I there? Usually, to get their money. Often, also, to round them up as customers for subsequent business activity and relationships. Also, to build brand identity. And for any number of other reasons. But foremost, to get their money. When I get them to laugh, I have done so not to get laughter but to further the getting of their money. When I gain their acceptance for an idea, I have done so not to educate but to further the getting of their money. And so on. If I get giant applause, love, people gathered for autographs, that's nifty, as long as it didn't interfere with the getting of their money. When I return home and am asked, "How did it go, dear?" I never answer with the number of minutes the ovation lasted or the number who wanted to take photos with me but with the total amount of money I removed from the room. If that sounds callous, try understanding it as a distinction between doing something as a professional for a professional purpose and doing something as an amateur absent such purpose. A weekend duffer might answer the "How did it go, dear?" question by saying he and the guys had a great time on the course, Bob hooked it through a car window, we lucked out with great weather, and a good time was had by all. A pro golfer answers with his score.

It's important to understand how powerful is clarity of purpose. If you step into a one-to-many selling situation without clarity to yourself; cluttered, crowded, conflicting agenda; worried over the looks on their faces; trying not to offend, being liked, getting applause, pleasing a meeting planner, getting accolades from peers, etc., you may very well achieve a number of those objectives *at expense of the response that counts*: sign-ups for appointments or order forms turned in at the rear of the room.

There is only one measurement of effectiveness for me. I live and die by sales, not lines for autographs, thank-yous, or ovations but *money*. Don't show me love, folks, show me the *money*. Jim Rohn once told me how he treasured the testimonial letters he received. I do too, but I treasure the treasure a lot more. A decade ago I said, were I in charge of rescuing Iraq, we'd own the oil. Trump has said the same thing in 2015. Not going to be beloved anyway; might as well get the oil. As a speaker, I know full well I'll be forgotten pretty quickly by 80 or 90% of the audience—a hand dipped into and pulled out of a pail of water. Might as well get their money.

If you are not directly selling, but more promoting your business, the same principle should apply. Instead of an order form and handing over of money, there should always be completion of some kind of form and making of some kind of commitment. To paraphrase Zig, being a professional *visitor* doesn't pay nearly as well as being a professional *salesman*—difference being signatures on dotted lines. That's the only way you should measure your success.

To say it from a different starting point, consider that crafting a speech and then performing in front of an audience delivering that speech are complex undertakings, for which there can be many measurements of *general* effectiveness. The same is true with, say, writing, producing, and putting out a movie. For the movie, there are reviews, awards—reflecting peer approval, even how the actors and you feel about the finished work. But there is only one *specific* measurement: box office. Walt Disney said, "Moviemakers are often too introverted about their productions . . . I am not influenced by the techniques or fashions of any other motion picture company or by any critics . . . in the making of a Disney movie, one essential is clarity . . . I don't really like to think about money that much, and I think about it most when I don't have enough to finance my latest enthusiasm, but everything we do must be done to be profitable; that has to be the governing principle: will the public support this with their money?"

If you'd like to be let off the hook on this, you *can* speak as a hobby or pastime or community service, or just to speak because you like speaking. When the results really don't matter, any results will do, so clarity of purpose and clarity of business purpose can be set aside. This is a little like playing Monopoly without the money, rolling dice, moving around and around the board without taking any properties or accumulating any money. If you are truly clear that you are doing that and want to do that, fine. This is why Harvey Penick called golf "a good walk, *spoiled*." For some, accurate measurement of successful achievement spoils everything. But if you want to succeed at using speaking to build a career or business, to attract patrons, or to directly sell, then clarity of purpose is required, and only one focal purpose will do.

CHAPTER 8

The Top Four Success Factors

T*he* number-one success factor is not skill or talent, style, voice, or content. It is definitely *not* academic credentials— to the distress of PhDs the world over. It isn't even being in front of the right audience, although that's quite helpful. It is:

THE #1 SUCCESS FACTOR

No guilt, no shame.

A lot of people, including people who like to think of themselves as *professional* speakers, are embarrassed about selling or selling aggressively from the platform. Never mind that, other than celebrities who are put on display like zoo animals and paid for who they are, not for what they say, all top-income speakers have been great and unabashed platform salespeople. Personally, for more than twenty years I *averaged* over $50,000 per speech. One of my most vocal critics, and vocal critic of all speakers selling from the platform within the National Speakers Association, privately confessed to me he was so critical of the practice because he had tried doing it and failed miserably.

If you are embarrassed by selling on stage, the audience senses it and *then* finds it objectionable and responds poorly to it.

There's no reason to be guilty about this either. Some pros critical of the practice argue that you should because you're being paid a fee and then abusing client and audience by taking time you've been paid for to use for your own purposes. There's a lengthy explanation of all the ways this is stupid in my book/course on the speaking business, *Big Mouth, Big Money*. Here I'll just make one point: the fee and the selling combined are the compensation for the speaking. In nonprofessional settings, where your only compensation is the promotion of your business or sale of your products or services, this shouldn't even enter your thoughts. Speaking-to-sell cannot be done timidly or worriedly or apologetically.

Being seen that way about anything you do, incidentally, is suicide. The day I was rock-solid certain Mitt Romney's presidential bid was dead, I saw him speak and talk about how Ann bought his dress shirts in three-packs at Costco. He was apologetic about his wealth. Voters will accept and elect rich people; they do it regularly. But they won't elect somebody who acts as if he is ashamed of it and afraid of negative reactions to it. The same exact truth applies to speaking-to-sell. There will often be a few in an audience who find it objectionable, and that must be a *so what?—tough shit*. But if you give off a vibe of feeling badly about it, you pour blood in the water, and the entire audience will want to kill you.

In a broader sense, people carry a lot of shame around for being peddlers and merchants or for having to be peddlers and merchants— when momma is prouder of their brother who's a doctor at Mount Sinai. People also lug around a lot of guilt for doing very well financially via something as grimy and low-on-totem-pole and societally unimportant as selling. They slap on a smile and a shoeshine each morning, but inside, they feel *dirty*.

This negative self-image really asserts itself when the person is doing the selling on stage, in the glare of the public spotlight, to 50 at the Rotary Club or 500 at a workshop. To this person, with these deep-seated emotional allergies to success, influence, and wealth earned by selling, the difference between doing "the dirty act" in private, one on one, across desk or table versus on stage in front of an audience must be similar to the prostitute performing in anonymity and privacy with one client behind curtains at the Holiday Inn versus filming an orgy scene, having sex with a horde of guys, in front of a camera crew, and having it plastered all over the Internet. There's dirty, and then there's *really, really dirty*. If this is what's running around inside your inner thoughts about self, selling, and speaking, no training in mechanics of these acts, no amount of practice speaking to mirror or dog, *nothing* will get you to proficiency.

It is beyond the scope of this book to sell you on selling as a noble, necessary profession there is every reason to be proud of and no reason to be ashamed of and that getting paid as much as you possibly can for use of your developed skills is also noble as well as appropriate. I refer you to two of my books: *No BS Wealth Attraction in the New Economy* and *No BS Sales Success in the New Economy*. Combined, they cost less than fifteen minutes with most shrinks.

Selling successfully, one-to-one, and more so, one-to-many requires a certain *personal* belief system—including end justifies means; your manipulation of your audience is okay because you are acting in their best interests; you are a professional deserving of top compensation; money is not finite, so what you take is not at the expense of others; and more. There are items that must be in your personal belief system that you would not trust others using, much like you might own a handgun but you wouldn't want your hot-tempered, alcoholic neighbor or your nine-year-old kid to have one.

There's no point to having a handgun at your bedside to protect yourself and spouse if you won't aim and fire when need arises, without hesitation. There's no point in constructing a magnificent sales speech and learning how to deliver it if you don't construct the essential belief system that allows you to use it.

Finally, remember that neither shame nor guilt comes with you from the womb. You create it for yourself based on your own thinking, attitudes, and acceptance of others' thinking and attitudes about every aspect of life. Shame and guilt are used by individuals, religions, and governments to manipulate you for their own purposes. In fact, both are tools of selling, too.

Ultimately, the belief system you construct for yourself about your purpose and rights when you step on stage in front of an audience will have far more to do with the money you walk away with than any other factor.

Just for the record, personally, when I speak-to-sell I speak-to-sell. I have no curiosity about whether or not I am removing someone's last dollar from their pocket and making them go hungry—I didn't make them poor. I have no qualms, no hesitations, no concern over criticism, no care about being liked, and utter disinterest in ovation, and nothing stands in my way of selling. I am entirely comfortable with what I am and entirely focused on why I am there. I am ruthless without remorse, in doing everything I can to extract every possible dollar from the greatest number of people present. I am self-interest in suit and tie. Woe be to the person who, in any way, interferes with my ability to achieve the highest possible sales. They will get my wrath. I am proud of my success at this and enraged at myself any time sales results are less than I've determined they should be. I am satisfied that I am providing greater potential value in what I am selling than the price I am taking for it, and I need no more justification than that. *I want your money.*

In context of performance, a comedian is there to *make* people laugh. Key word: *make*. Not timidly offer ideas and invite people to choose which they might find amusing. Not to submit to critique. To make them laugh. A magician is there to *make* people believe in his illusions. I am there to *make* them hand over their money.

THE #2 SUCCESS FACTOR

No fear.

No one has been hung in this country for speaking since the early 1900s. As a common practice, it ended before then. Careers do end because of something said—think comedian Michael Richards or radio host Don Imus. Imus returned after a period of exile to the Farm Radio Network but in lesser form. Ultimately, he made his way all the way back before retiring. But one thing said sent him from top of mountain to ghetto. As of this writing, Richards has not been seen since his little meltdown in a comedy club, filled with racial vitriol. The more popular Tracy Morgan fared better with his homophobic remarks problem but had to do a lot of groveling. In June or July of 2011, a frequent guest pundit on MSNBC responded to a query about his opinion of President Obama's press conference by saying, "Well, I think he was kind of a dick." He was immediately suspended by MSNBC. President Bush the first, with "Read my lips.

No new taxes." Oops. But by and large, tens of thousands of people give interviews, press conferences and speeches, many for commercial purposes, every single day and escape lynching or even minor bodily harm. You'll probably get out alive. And almost every venue has an exit by the stage and a back door. If it worries you, write it into your contract.

You simply can't speak-to-sell afraid—of anything, including someone taking offense.

I offend people nearly every time I speak, I've given nearly 2,500 compensated presentations over thirty-five or so years and only once been accosted and verbally assaulted in a threatening manner by anybody. And she was a 5'5" Avon sales manager. I could have taken her.

Okay, if you're not in fear of your life, what *are* you afraid of? Generally, people who fear speaking fear embarrassment and humiliation, being poorly received, maybe being heckled. People who speak-to-sell fear being disliked or criticized for, in fact, selling. All these fears are 100% legitimate. In fact, they're nearly inevitable. If you're saying much of anything and, especially, if you are selling, you will be disliked and criticized for it by some, probably consistently. You may find yourself poorly received by an entire audience someplace. You may even have some incident that causes you some embarrassment. All these things will happen. But, fortunately, they are also utterly irrelevant.

A speech is a blip in your lifetime. If you are poorly received or disliked or even embarrassed, so what? Will it matter in thirty-six hours? Thirty-six days? Thirty-six weeks? Thirty-six months? *Pfui.* When I started speaking I was far, far, far from good. Nearly embarrassingly bad. No scars. No lasting impact. It'll be over in less time than a winter cold. As humiliations go, a joke failing to get laughs or people leaving while you're talking is pretty damn minor. Compared, say, to Tiger Woods' entire year of 2010 or Obama's entire presidency, it's a mosquito bite.

As to being disliked or criticized for selling while speaking, again, so what, so what, so what? What matters *is* selling. So *the buyers* matter. Everyone else, unless you play canasta with them every Thursday, screw 'em. Anybody successfully, visibly making a boatload of money, or in many quarters even a little money, is going to be deeply resented and criticized by many. Their stated objections are bullshit. Their envy is palpable and real. Their power to do you any real harm, virtually nil. So they are no more real than a six-year-old's entirely imagined bogeymen beneath the bed. Personally, I find these folks whose delicate sensibilities are so pained by my making money in front of them pathetically predictable and mildly amusing. It's like watching monkeys at the zoo. You know they're going to throw their feces, but it's still funny.

Two requisites for success, selling from the platform: one, being perfectly okay with it yourself, and two, being perfectly okay that some will be very un-okay with it.

THE #3 SUCCESS FACTOR

Total, unwavering clarity of purpose—and a willingness to sacrifice any and all to achieve it.

We've already beat this one up, but guess what?—I'm going to beat it up some more.

You have to reverse engineer the entire speech itself for strategic purposes. You may have a story or a joke you tell well and are in love with and know audiences respond well to, but if it doesn't advance the cause and contribute to the objective of the speech, it should stay at home on the shelf. You have to deliver the speech and control everything around the delivery of the speech, in the way that will achieve your chief focal objective. Doing anything else is irresponsible.

In my own speaking career—in which I rose to the very top of the profession—I had occasional tussles with meeting planners, occasionally left an annoyed meeting planner afterward, and often offended people in my audiences, all to achieve my chief objective: attracting to me however many ideally suited customers or clients there were in each audience. Magnetically raising the gold needles out of the haystack. Everyone else could go pound sand. The harsh reality is that, in order to resonate with targeted clientele, you have to be profoundly disliked by others. The speaker liked by all is, days later, remembered by few and draws even fewer to him, foaming at the mouth to give him big stacks of money for whatever he has to offer. Clarity about *this* is vital. Clear thinking about the need for being polarizing, *not* popular, is significant, and for many folks, difficult.

Beware competing objectives. It's hard to serve multiple masters well. Getting standing ovations, getting peer approval, winning awards, not risking offending, and so on—each is an objective, as is my own of being magnetic to certain people in an audience, selling a ton of stuff, and signing up a lot of customers. In most cases, these objectives conflict. You must choose and be clear about your choice and prepared for and okay with its ramifications.

THE #4 SUCCESS FACTOR

Structure.

A speech that sells is *not* a speech that does other things with a commercial tacked onto its ass like pin the tail on the donkey—a very common mistake.

Most speeches that sell well are engineered from the start and throughout to set up and make the sale. They are structured like a sales presentation or a written sales letter, leading a prospect step by step, thought by thought, to the point of buying. They use the kind of sales formulas found in my book *The Ultimate Sales Letter.* Usually, there are a few key ideas—and there should only be a few—that you seek audience grasp of, that stack, establishing need and desire for what is being sold. That looks like this:

In my speech selling *Magnetic Marketing*®: (1) What you're doing now to get customers is frustrating, hit-or-miss, costly, making you weary and sick. (2) It's not your fault: everybody but me, everybody who has led you to what you do now is an idiot or a charlatan. (3) There is a better way. There is a simple formula with three parts: message, market, media. (4) You need a compelling marketing message including at least a unique selling proposition and a call to action. (5) You need to target market to ideal prospects (not mass market like a goof). (6) You need to use media to deliver your message efficiently to your target market—look at this cool direct-mail example.

8   Versions of that speech are on a DVD included with my *Renegade Millionaire System*® and in other information products available at GKIC.com/store. If you'd like an abbreviated, written transcript of it, please send a self-addressed 9x12" envelope and a request to: Kennedy Inner Circle Inc., 15433 N. Tatum Blvd. #104, Phoenix, AZ 85032.

The agreements that this establishes are: (A) Yep, I'm not getting what I want out of advertising and marketing—he's right about that. (This is "Awareness.") (B) Gee, I am missing some key elements, so it's no wonder I'm not getting better results. (This is "Sense of Inadequacy.") (C) It'd be really great to have and use the kind of weapons he's talking about and showing. Then, from my bridge to perceived commercial, (D) He's right—I'll never remember all this or be able to do it just from my scribbled notes. It is (A)–(D) that sets up the sale of the *Magnetic Marketing System*® Tool Kit.

If, however, I delivered a really interesting and instructional speech about marketing not structurally engineered to get these four agreements, and I did not stack items (1)–(6) on top of each other as foundation and wasn't able to refer back to them during the core commercial, and then just tacked a pitch for the product on the end, *I would fail.*

Let me be *very* clear. I sold more per event and outearned by the year quite a few professional speaker peers who were much better speakers per se than I was or am now. I did not accomplish this by pre-existing fame; many were more famous than I was. I did not accomplish this by circumstances; we sold in the same venues to the same people. I did not accomplish this by talent; I have little—just highly developed, purposed skill. I accomplished this by the specific success factors in this chapter, including, importantly, the structure of my speeches.

So, think about this for some sort of local, professional practice, with a speech intended to motivate people to book appointments and come into the office. (1) You are in grave and imminent danger from hidden gum disease, from Obama's financial reform, etc. and your ability to live safely and joyously or as a sick/poor creature depends on how you handle this. (2) Everything you've read, been told, etc., is wrong, and your doctors, accountant, etc., have let you down. (3) There is a better way. (4) You need "x." (5) Here's what "x" looks like. The agreements are: (A) Yep, I fit the bill, I'm at risk, I had no idea before how close to the cliff's edge of debilitating illness, death, or poverty I am. (B) I can see that I don't have "a," and I'm not doing "b." (C) I would be happier, healthier, wealthier if I had these things. (D) I damn sure can't do all this for myself.

Obviously, there are a number of other elements that need to be worked in or overlaid or in place in advance of the speech. The local professional needs to be established as authority figure and celebrity, needs to create trust, needs to be likable, etc. In selling my info-product, I, too, need established authority and celebrity, I have to erase certain common objections, I have to present price. But what is not situational, that is universally true, is that *the entire speech needs to be structured to sell.*

THIS IS NOT "PERFORMANCE ART." THIS IS *SELLING.*

Most speakers don't get this—and if they do, they don't like it. They want to be spontaneous. I saw the great producer Andrew Lloyd Webber (Phantom of the Opera; Evita) interviewed by Piers Morgan and asked what he thought about the remarkable vocal talent revealed by Susan Boyle for a lead role in a Broadway musical. He said, paraphrasing, she can sing like the dickens, but I don't think she can be disciplined enough to sing the same songs precisely the same way throughout eight shows a week for 104 or 156 consecutive weeks. The great sales speakers do exactly that. Speech structure to script and strict self-discipline to perform it as structured and scripted is the mark of a *professional* speaker who sells.

Most speakers don't get this—and if they do, they don't like it. They want to teach, inspire, be thought of as brilliant, and get standing ovations. Sane individuals know it's a practical impossibility to imbed significant knowledge let alone skill and alter behavior in sixty or ninety minutes or even days, so the sale of resources and tools to people made aware of opportunity is *the only ethical approach and the only really worthy accomplishment*—therefore, doing that the very best way it can be done so as to put those resources in the hands of as many people as possible is the highest integrity; doing it poorly because of personal preferences, ego, etc. is the lowest integrity. Sales speakers could care less about standing ovations. We measure success by stampedes to buy. Our measurement is legitimate, by the way. It's easy to manipulate an audience into giving a standing ovation even to an utterly worthless speech delivered by a lousy speaker. After all, it costs the audience nothing to give it, and it gets them up and that much closer to out the door. If they invest their money or otherwise commit to next steps, well, that's something. Speech structure to script and strict self-discipline to perform it as structured and scripted is the way speakers who sell achieve desired results.

Most speakers don't get this—and if they do, they don't like it. They haven't gotten good at structuring sales conversations and act in undisciplined ways in their business life offstage, so why would they want to structure their work onstage? People are sloppy. Lazy. Uninformed. Ill-prepared. If you are going to speak-to-sell successfully, you are going to learn how to sell, study selling, prepare and practice a great sales speech, exercise influence if not control over the preparation of the audience, meticulously dress for your performance, be extremely disciplined in language, tone, pace, gesture. Speech structure to script and strict self-discipline to perform it as structured and scripted is the mark of a professional speaker who sells.

When Woody Allen said that a third of all success is just showing up, he was 33% right. Just getting out there, up in front of groups, just visibility, will promote your business and will ferret some great buyers, customers, or clients out of a population. Conversely, knowing your stuff like nobody else on earth but staying at home with your cat is unlikely to attract much prosperity into your life. In my book *No BS Wealth Attraction in the New Economy*, I lay out twenty-eight Wealth Magnets. Three of them are: Be Somebody, Be Somewhere, and Do Something. Sounds simple, yet it's a powerful triangle-formula few consistently practice. But it is still, basically, only the 33% Woody Allen identified. Structure and the self-discipline to perform within the structure engineered for desired results is a major step from activity to purposeful, productive accomplishment.

Copyright © Dan Kennedy 2007 Vincent Palko www.AdToons.com

From the book, *No BS Time Management For Entrepreneurs* by Dan Kennedy.

CHAPTER 9

Masquerade

"All the world's a stage, and we are but players . . ."

—Shakespeare

In the business of prostitution, *I have been told* there is a thing called GFE—Girlfriend Experience. It refers to an escort acting as if there's a real date, a real relationship, possibly even going out to dinner and theater or weekend together along with, of course, having sex. For the client, it's fantasy. For the hooker, it's a masquerade. She is there for only two real reasons: to get money and to get as much money as possible. There are other kinds of masquerades role-played by women in this profession. Ask Client #9 a.k.a. former New York governor Eliot Spitzer, who made his bones prosecuting the very same businesses of this ilk that he privately patronized. The governor spent a lot of money on masquerades held for his benefit.

Disney World is a very happy place . . . sloganized as the "Happiest Place On Earth." It is also the business most closely operated by the strategies in my *No BS Ruthless Management of People & Profits (2nd Edition)*. Key word: *ruthless*. At Disney World, there is a script for everything, defined procedures, tough standards, micromanagement of sales by place and person and time of day, ever-present mystery shopping, rigid enforcement, the pressure of huge financial burden and high expectations. What guests see is an epic masquerade, concealing determined military precision applied to moneymaking.

Most workplaces are places of masquerade. People pretend to be earnest members of the team while secretly shopping for a better job or stealing supplies or playing Angry Birds on company time, another form of theft. People pretend to like each other while scheming to get each other fired. Most businesses, like Disney, present themselves as one thing to the public while, concealed behind closed doors, they have a very different business. Sometimes you can peel away layer after layer as with an onion. The MLM or network marketing industry is a fascinating example of this—there is the business the public thinks the company is in, related to its products; the business the rank and file distributors think it's in—recruiting distributors and helping them develop successful businesses; the business the tiny, elite fraternity of top distributors know they are in; and the real business the company's owners are in. The secrets can be partially divined with a few facts: less than 10% of the product is ever sold at retail to consumers who are not distributors; fewer than 5% of all the "active" distributors purchasing product every month are at or ever reach significant income, fewer than 1% a six-figure income; top distributors sell their own and other top distributors' audio and video programs, sales aids, web sites, training seminars, and coaching outside the MLM compensation system. Even given these facts, most can't totally decipher all the code without help of a knowledgeable insider. But you can realize there's a lot more hidden than visible. There's a masquerade being played out.

Next time you're out to dinner, look at the couple at a nearby table obviously on a date but not married; you know how to tell. Consider. She is wearing Spanx underneath her dress and a padded, push-up bra enhancing cleavage, has artificially plumped her lips and masked wrinkles, has dyed her hair, and is ordering less food or lesser-priced food than she would like or a salad that can be primly eaten rather than the messy ribs she would prefer. He is wearing man-Spanx, has lifts in his shoes, has lied about the importance of his job to suggest a greater income than he earns, and is feigning interest in her story about whatever. The whole evening is a masquerade.

Many moons back, my friend Lee Milteer, then single, told me she was inviting a man she was interested in over for dinner. I said: false advertising. There was a kitchen there only because it came with the house. (Just because every car I've ever bought came equipped with a spare tire doesn't mean I can or will change a tire.) How many such masquerades are happening all across America tonight?

Most families are masquerades. There are happy group photos in scrapbooks and on Facebook. Not shown: scheming, undermining, backstabbing, infidelity, jealousy, resentment, sibling rivalry, and—revealed by divorce or a death—war over money. More *Dallas* than *Leave It to Beaver*. This does not mean that family isn't a worthy institution important and beneficial to its members and to society as a whole or that family members aren't bonded to each other in a unique way. It just means that most families are not what they seem to be or present themselves to be.

Most churches are masquerades. When the collection plate is passed, a mood has been created, a sermon rich with imbedded sales-manship, emotional manipulation, and subliminal commands has been given, peer pressure is visibly applied, and starving orphans or construction of hospitals in distant lands or some such eleemosy-nary initiative invoked—with no mention made of how much of the money is paying for salaries, overhead, travel, being routed to "the home office," then invested in real estate, stocks, bonds, loaned to build casinos, and so on. Were that disclosure statement required by law, that Sunday selling job would be a lot tougher. This does not mean, however, that churches aren't worthy institutions benefi-cial to their parishioners and charitable to others and a good and useful force within society. It just means they aren't what they present themselves as. Having actually taken over a public company with a Catholic diocese as its third largest creditor and having done business with those folks, having conducted marketing training for ministers back in the 1980s—that predated but was very much in sync with Pastor Rick Warren's current business book for ministers, *The Purpose-Driven Church*, which is must reading for any marketer—and having gotten to know several mega-church ministers, I can guarantee you that what the parishioners see on Sunday is an orchestrated masquer-ade concealing a great deal they would never want to know about. A week as a fly on the wall in the business meetings of a church would have the same effect on a devout believer as a behind-the-scenes tour of a hog farm and sausage factory has on a lady who cooks bacon and eggs every morning for her family.

With all this, I have journeyed far, wide, and long to make the simple point that *everything is masquerade.* Any queasiness about orchestrating and performing your own masquerade will render you ineffectual in a marketplace that *requires it.*

Speaking-to-sell is a masquerade. A Kabuki dance of sorts. The audience is led to believe you care about them. You feign delivery of a great deal of valuable information and instruction they can use. In reality, you meticulously craft the presentation to appear to be useful but to actually only arouse desire so that they will want what is being sold to them. You care about the ones who buy and about their future value as customers. *They are, in fact, having one experience; you are having a different experience.* Evil? I think only if what you are selling is, itself, a lie. Otherwise, it's no worse a masquerade than all the other masquerades of daily life. The reality concealed—that is, your reality—does not in any way diminish the satisfaction they get from their experience.

The best analogy of all those given here compares speaking-to-sell to the prostitute's performance if providing the Girlfriend Experience. You might think that a very unflattering comparison, but I have no emotional response to it one way or the other, and I see it as accurate and therefore instructive. She and I both perpetrate illusion, utilize the principle of distraction, rely on choreographed and practiced performance, and have a mercenary purpose. I deliver the Cared For, Motivated, and Educated Audience Member Experience, she delivers the Girlfriend Experience. Arguably, I deliver more useful value after the fact, by sending some audience members out the door invested in my resources that may pay monetary and other dividends in the future, while she leaves only a memory. Value is subjective and property of recipient, though, and isn't relevant here, anyway; we're just working at understanding exactly what we're doing when speaking-to-sell. That's what I'm getting at: an honest, rational, and accurate understanding of what you are doing when speaking-to-sell.

If you are selling on behalf of your local business, you won't be collecting all their wallets and getting out of town before the posse forms—as I did, a lot, for a lot of years. You have to live with these people afterward, day in and day out. In fact, you want to, because your business model requires it. This does not fundamentally alter anything I just said about what you are really doing on small or large stage, speaking to promote your business. You *aren't* there to *actually* educate them to the point of *actually* being able to go and do anything for themselves without patronizing your business, yet you probably want them to have a feeling of being educated, better informed, and more knowledgeable. You *aren't* there to entertain them or to be entertaining, although you may very well be entertaining for a sales purpose. For maximum influence, your performance will be perceived as all about one thing but will secretly be about something else.

A lot of people will find this idea—likely this whole book—objectionable, because it is so much about psychological and emotional manipulation. You may feel that you shouldn't have to manipulate someone's inner child and deep-seated fears and negative emotions and emotional scars and unmet desires and engage in masquerade in order to sell them something. If something is beneficial to them, and you present the facts in a credible way, that *should* be enough. If something is valuable to them, you *should* be able to lay out that value and simply state the price. All this presumes that people act with the free will given them as birthright and that they are rational beings—both presumptions false, dangerous, and, ironically, based on what you, yourself, *feel* and *believe* about the way things ought to be, not about rational assessment of the way things are.

In speaking, you are engaged in a schizophrenic and partly secretive activity. You are creating an experience for the audience and certain satisfying perceptions by the audience, but you are also conducting a carefully engineered sales presentation almost certainly including some level of psychological and emotional manipulation—preferably unnoticed in large part or whole—leading the audience to *your* predetermined objective. In speaking-to-sell, that objective is having them buy.

This is *all* about your objective.

In, say, a seventy-five-minute speech there might be ten minutes of overt selling, where there's no masquerade, describing what you get and what you pay—and it's these ten minutes the audience will perceive as "the commercial" or, uncharitably, the sales pitch. But actually, you will have engineered the entire seventy-five minutes as a sales presentation, creating desire and then serving up its solution via every word, story, example, gesture. If they got information, they got information helpful to the sale and presented for that (real) reason— not presented for information's sake. Never forget: schoolteachers and professors make a lot less money than good salesmen.

CHAPTER 10

Toastmasters, Not So Much

Y ou have undoubtedly heard the most basic speaking advice: tell 'em what you're going to tell 'em, tell 'em, then tell 'em what you told them. Limited to three ideas. Separated by stories. Yada yada. Oh, and stand up straight, project your voice, wear clean underwear, and don't put your hands in your pockets.

This may get you through a Dale Carnegie class and might get you an award in a Toastmasters group. But when you speak-to-sell, the game afoot is much more manipulative. You are not just putting ideas across, you are reaching into peoples' psyches and pulling out their wallets. Again, there are vast differences between speaking, speaking to broadly influence, speaking (just) to establish authority and reputation, and speaking-to-sell. The "by-the-book stuff" isn't up to the task of moving people to immediate action, particularly buying action. That doesn't negate structure fundamentals. I tend to use a 3x3 structure myself: three acts, like a three-act play, each conveying three key concepts. These are bracketed: at the start, a preface of promises, telling the audience where we're going; and at the end, a summary, then a bridge to the sale when selling. Structure may be very similar from purpose to purpose, but what gets delivered within the structure definitely is not. A lot of what is done to speak-to-sell would be criticized and run afoul of the norms of the lecture intended to illuminate or inspire.

I am sometimes dubbed "The Professor of Harsh Reality." This is the harshest chapter in this entire book. Brace yourself.

BRING THE PAIN

In speaking-to-sell, we tap into, arouse, and manipulate *negative* emotions. We create a *negative* mental state that only our product relieves and solves. For this reason, I always cringe when I'm referred to as a "motivational speaker." More accurately, I am a pain-inducing, sense-of-inadequacy-inducing, fear-inducing, anger-inducing, resentment-inducing speaker. I'm damn good at it and, privately, proud of it.

If you closely examine my most famous multi-million-dollar speech used to sell my *Magnetic Marketing System®*, you'll find quite a bit of this. I pigeonhole the business owners in the audience as advertising *victims*; I denigrate the sales professionals for doing old-fashioned, primitive, dirty, ugly cold prospecting—like coal mining. I make sure everybody feels inadequate because they don't have a USP, because they are doing dumb, "throw mud against the wall" marketing instead of target marketing, because they don't leverage media. I remind them they are going to sleep at night worrying because they have no system in place assuring them of new customers coming in the next day and every day. *I beat them up a lot* in seventy-five minutes. Even with my wrap-up story, which has a lot of humor in it, I get them to compare themselves to a lowly plumber who is much more sophisticated about his marketing and selling than they are. My bridge to my product presentation is about how inadequate and flawed their minds and memories are—thus they will have wasted their time with me and will continue as a marketing incompetent without my take-home resources.

Tearing people down, prodding inadequacy, and making them feel "small" is not normally done in ordinary informational or inspirational speeches, but it is a vital part of a speech that sells. Along with it, some level of pugnacity helps, too. Even seemingly gentle speakers, like the paternal Zig Ziglar, play these cards. Zig, for example, shamed people guilty of what he called stinkin' thinkin'.

He has stinkin' thinking.

From the book *Make 'Em Laugh and Take Their Money* by Dan Kennedy.

It's *not* exactly the EST seminar, which began with, **"You are all assholes. *Your* life *doesn't* work. I am your trainer because *my* life *does* work."** But the principle in play *is* exactly the same. (EST, incidentally, was, in its time, by far, the biggest and most successful "human potential" seminar company, birthed by Werner Erhard, a once and former vacuum cleaner salesman and MLM operator. It was a national sensation.)

With a speech like mine, most people aren't fully aware that they've been deliberately, methodically, emotionally brutalized and made to feel dumb and inept as a precursor to buying that which will make them smart and able. They hear it and feel it, but they usually don't detect the intent or extent of the manipulation. This *can* be done with a certain degree of subtlety. With some humor. With varying style and tone. But it *needs* to be done.

I have just handed you a very powerful formula. Succinct. Simple. Create burning despair, *then* burning desire.

Until this writing, I've never gone this far in explaining the intended psychological manipulation engineered into my best sales speeches. It's been there to see for those who could see it, and I've gone right up to the edge of revealing it but stopped a few feet short. So this is something special, here in this book, written very late in my career, when I very seldom speak-to-sell anymore. I will tell you that, over the years, I've built more than fifty sales speeches for myself and others that have been worth at least one million dollars each, and every single one of them has had this same psychological core: making people feel bad, making them feel dumb, inept, victimized, and inadequate.

You may not find that *noble*. I made peace with it very early, with good ends for all justifying my means—and because I care far more about achieving the best possible results than I do anything else. If you can't get to the same place, you'll be severely handicapped in selling from the stage. Sorry. **You may judge it as *cynical*.** I see it as pragmatic understanding of human psychology, thus neither good nor bad, positive or negative. One of the least-liked success secrets is dealing with things and people as they actually are. Another is doing what is necessary to get the best results, without labeling or judging what that is. It's all just what it is. Nothing more or less. **You may think of me as a monster** as you read the above paragraphs. It's okay; what you think of me doesn't matter to me. But what you decide to think about this will matter a lot to you—and, ironically, to the people you might help or benefit by your influence and by what you sell. Most won't benefit if treated gently and nicely.

Most people do *not* move much by promise of positive benefit or gain, by paths shown to improvement. We all think *we* do, but the reality is that more and sharper-felt provocation is usually involved when someone makes an attitudinal or behavioral change of almost any sort or invests money in doing so. That provocation is most often some form of *pain*. If you want to move the sales needle, stick it in hard and twist it. As I write this, the current, number-one television commercial for an animal charity is so harsh, gruesome, and sad, the voice over it quickly acknowledges you'll want to turn away from it. It is *tough*. The best food charity pitch I ever wrote made the reader absolutely ashamed and guilty for their big Thanksgiving dinner. People put in pain over their own blessings are easily induced to relieve the pain by a donation. People shown the happy kids or safe animals made possible by donations are not nearly as responsive. This principle—and it is a *principle*—applies perfectly to speaking-to-sell. The speaker has a relatively short time and a high, high hurdle: he can't settle for conceptual agreement, acceptance of ideas, positive feelings, or applause. He needs a big leap to immediate action.

We don't want just influence. We want *undue influence*: outsized influence. *Actual* authority: the ability to prescribe, and to be so feared and respected and surrendered to that our prescriptions are complied with. We don't want to influence exercise of free will—we want to replace their free will with our will. Commandeering actual authority is much more about dark arts than light touch.

All religion, incidentally, is structured from the ground up in this same way, so that control can be imposed based on the followers' sense of inadequacy and failure. If you can bring yourself to logically think through the Ten Commandments, you'll acknowledge that no human can go a full week without violating at least a few of them, and *that is the point*—without the ability to persistently remind people they are sinners, how would the collection plates be filled? The angelic President Jimmy Carter confessed, in a *Playboy Magazine* interview of all places, to reoccurring lust in his heart and said that, in his mind, that was just as sinful as actually committing adultery. One wonders if all his pounding of nails for Habitat for Humanity would have gone on were he entirely free of guilt. I choose not to think of God as a sadistic fiend enjoying all this as entertainment, like a cat toying with a helpless mouse, so if he did actually author the big ten, I'll give him credit for the same kind of good-end-for-all-justifies-the-means decisions as my own. Before you trouble yourself sending me angry letters or religious pamphlets, I am *not* passing critical judgment on any religion or deity or belief system held by any follower with what I just said. I am only asking you to be briefly objective and analytical, to see how authority is created, exerted, and sustained. And understand the psychological tools chosen, which work. In 2015, the Pope made a lot of news with his visit to America and a myriad of criticisms of American capitalism and culture, which were defended by him and his spokespersons by explaining that **his job was to *make people uncomfortable.***

So I will briefly tell you why I felt and feel just fine about playing this game to win. First, I've never sold anything that wouldn't be beneficial and valuable far beyond its cost to every purchaser who actually used it—and I've never accepted any responsibility for those sabotaging themselves with the sin of sloth, who don't use it. Second, I've always detested everything required to get to speak, so I was determined to extract the greatest possible amount of money (Present Bank and Future Bank money) from every such workday and have always felt I earned every penny. Third, I am a realist about humans; I know they cannot be expected to act in their best interests based on simple logic and facts or irrefutable and clear demonstration of value; nearly their every decision and act comes by others' manipulation. Thus, adding one, two, and three together, I conclude that should I "go easy" on the manipulation, I write myself a smaller paycheck than was available but do no one any good via my sacrifice.

One other thing: I've never been bothered by my audiences not knowing what just happened to them after I've finished. That's the nature of everything: the food served to them in restaurants, which they thoroughly enjoy, is provided absent required viewing of a DVD presentation of the butchering of the animals or even a close inspection of the cooking in the kitchen. If you now have a good marriage, know it occurred because neither one of you engaged in full disclosure during the sales process. If you benefit by being a Catholic, your faith would probably be destroyed if you sat in on all the high-level meetings at the Vatican for a month—and the same would be true of every other organized religious institution. If you knew what your dog actually thinks of you, you might not sleep easily at night. You might very well enjoy my next speech less now knowing its schematic. I view speaking *and* speaking-to-sell as a structured process that benefits the audience, and having them fully grasp what is being done, why, and how does not contribute to their benefit. So, as the saying goes, what they don't know won't hurt them.

If all this troubles you deeply and makes you want to go take a shower, I actually do understand, and I do not have a negative opinion of you because of it. But I have a harsh suggestion. Money getting is just not a suitable occupation for the faint of heart or gentle of soul. And there are plenty of other ways to make a living, so if this talks you out of speaking-to-sell because you just haven't got the stomach for it, that might be a good thing. The Salvation Army needs a few good men, and you don't have to understand how incredibly manipulative their fund-raising is to don an apron and dish out soup to the homeless.

CHAPTER 11

National Speakers Association, Not So Much

Should you be a professional or aspiring professional speaker and find your way to membership in the National Speakers Association, there is much to be gained—but there is also great hazard.

First, linked to my comments about masquerades in chapter 9, this thing is not at all what it seems to be on the surface. It is more akin to the mass delusion of the multilevel-marketing industry than it is to a legitimate trade association. In a trade association or the GKIC association that I created, the majority of members are actually in the businesses they say they are in and earning at least respectable incomes from those businesses. The members of the Florida Association of Independent Insurance Agents are nearly all real insurance agents and brokers, making real livings by selling insurance. The members of a state's dental association tend to be real dentists, most operating dental practices, most making a good living at it. Not so with NSA. NSA is largely populated with aspiring speakers, amateur speakers, part-timers with day jobs, college professors, rich doctors' wives, and assorted other *not-really*-professional speakers. Most of these are encouraged by NSA to think they are the minority, surrounded by a majority who are very successful, when the truth is the opposite. Further, a goodly number of the actual pros in the NSA population, including "names" you might know, make a whole lot less money than you'd imagine or they would admit to anyone but the IRS. They are a comparatively poor lot. If you compared the average income of the NSA-member speakers with the average income of the members of most real trade associations—chiropractors, dentists, veterinarians, restaurant owners, plumbers, etc.—you'd find the NSA average low on the totem pole. Again, this does not mean there isn't benefit to be had by participation. Just don't be too starry-eyed, and don't lose grip on the fact that NSA's chief purpose is perpetuation of NSA.

Second, there is a deeply ingrained cultural bias in NSA against selling, selling from the stage, exercising control over meeting planners, and even making a lot of money. You might think this odd for a group filled with "motivational speakers," but it permeates the environment like the odor in a neighborhood downwind from a steel mill or poultry plant. If you live there, you become immune to it and don't notice the stench. If you hang out too much with the NSA crowd and aren't critically discriminating about who you pay attention to and who you don't, you'll fail to notice the stench of failed premises and philosophical positions and delusional ideas, the odor of jealousy and resentment toward success. But it's there. Again, this does not mean there isn't benefit to be had by participation. Just don't lose grip on the fact that there is an ingrained, nearly theological bias toward simple fee-paid speaking and against speaking-to-sell; toward subservience to bureaus, agents, and meeting planners and against autonomy. You have to carefully sort out what you can use and what is poisonous to you. There's some of both.

The biggest thing to be wary of is the emphasis on the "art of" speaking and on what NSA culture defines as "being professional" as a speaker—on stage and in business dealings with clients, meeting planners, and promoters. There is a religious zealotry here for the long-antiquated proposition that if you just keep getting better and better and better at speaking, funnier, better at story telling, better at gestures, heck, better at breathing; if you create better content; if you ultimately *glow* up there, fame and fortune will beat a path to your door. Not only is this happy horseshit useful only in persuading people that their lack of progress financially is entirely the fault of their not being ready yet as a prime time performer and yet one more investment in getting better may finally awaken the world to their star quality, it gets squarely in the way of the things that really create fame and fortune.

To be fair about this, I *do* have a personal chip on my shoulder about NSA. In the interest of full disclosure, you should know it. Having raised myself up from fledgling, admittedly inept, and starving speaker to a hugely successful multi-decade career in speaking culminating with nine years in one of the most coveted speaking slots on the number one, largest, most famous public seminar tour in American history; consistently earning a seven-figure yearly income from speaking; having used my speaking to found and fuel a business ultimately becoming the largest of any speaker's businesses, encompassing five successful newsletters and other publishing, large international events, two membership associations, even a network of local chapters, and value so substantial it was acquired for a large sum by a successful private equity firm—something hardly any speaker has ever accomplished; and having consulted with and coached and assisted numerous speakers, I *resent* getting *zero* recognition from the association I stayed a member of for a long time. I fess up to that resentment.

Imagine this: one of the all-time most successful, most innovative leaders in a field being deliberately and totally ignored by his industry's association. Remarkable, I think. Imagine an association of TV producers telling Dick Wolf, the mastermind of the number one multi-show franchise in TV, *Law & Order*, "We're not really interested in what you might have to say about this business." Imagine an association of authors telling my friends Mark Victor Hansen and Jack Canfield, creators of the *Chicken Soup for the Soul* empire or J. K. Rowling, creator of Harry Potter, or the creators of the *For Dummies* books, "We're not really interested in what *you* might have to say about this business." So, yes, I harbor a grudge—and I'm Irish; a true Irishman with Alzheimer's forgets everything but his grudges. But chip on my shoulder or no chip, the fact is, had I been heavily influenced by the NSA culture's imperatives, "company line," and peer pressure, I would never have accomplished any of those things fueled by speaking-to-sell, that have given me a thirty-five-year tenure as prolific published author with audience and made me rich. Had I bought into the culture code that NSA promotes, I'd have been *crippled*. As it has crippled others.

To be entirely fair, a few very courageous NSA'ers have had me come in and speak at local NSA chapters. So, technically, I've not gone entirely without recognition in the NSA world. And a number of NSA leaders have taken it upon themselves to attend my seminars or retain me privately, to consult with them on their business. A past-president of NSA, enormously well respected within NSA (and a much more deft political fellow than I), Nido Qubein honored me with an honorary spot on the advisory board to the School of Communications at High Point University. One of my No BS books—on grassroots marketing for local businesses—is coauthored with Jeff Slutsky, a long-time NSA member well-liked within. Overall, members of NSA have spent at least a couple million dollars with me one way or another, looking to me for business guidance. Yet the association itself, as entity and as professional fraternity, has never so much as acknowledged my existence, let alone invited me to its main convention stage to tell the story of how speaking-to-sell can build an empire. Did I mention I have a chip on my shoulder? But enough about me.

As a general rule, *any* society where top sales producers are shunned or stigmatized, where illusion and delusion is preferred to reality, where the richest and most successful members aren't celebrated, and where businesspeople aren't businesslike should be participated in cautiously, skeptically, and in small doses.

With those caveats, I did say, up top, that NSA membership *could* be beneficial, at least briefly, and I meant it. Mostly because, unfortunately, it holds a monopoly. It is the only association of speakers and speaking business entrepreneurs. It is where people adept at speaking and knowledgeable about the ins and outs of getting speaking opportunities, using online media to do so, working with the convention industry, and other aspects of both "the art of"—which has some importance—and the business of speaking gather. Its convention always has *some* useful presenters and presentations, some useful exhibitors to be found, and, of course, the networking and eavesdropping and engaging in hallway, cocktail lounge, and poolside discussions—often the *most* useful thing of all. A number of great long-term relationships began for me within NSA. I am grateful Cavett Robert, Somers White, Bill Gove, and other earliest pros put it together and breathed life into it, grateful it existed, and appreciative of all it led me to.

I will also say, for useful business and moneymaking information, related to but not narrowed to speaking, the Information Marketing Association is a far more legitimate and trustworthy source, albeit a smaller entity. If you are not a member, visit info-marketing.org. Similarly, attending the annual Info-SUMMIT℠ hosted by GKIC and the Information Marketing Association is a more reality-based excursion. If the business of speaking interests you, then, for the real story, you must get my *Big Mouth, Big Money* program, from GKIC.com/store. Yes, this entire paragraph was a crass commercial announcement, inserted without remorse despite the fact you paid to get this book. They now make you watch commercials in a movie theater you bought a ticket to get into, too.

Looping all the way back to speaking-to-sell or to promote your business, Toastmasters *might* be a good place to gain some experience for the entirely inexperienced and unconfident speaker—but beware counterproductive indoctrination. The National Speakers Association *can* be a place to meet and rub elbows with and selectively form good relationships with other speakers—but beware counterproductive indoctrination. Your purpose for speaking will be different than most everybody you encounter in these worlds, so you have to carefully analyze whatever advice is offered through your unique prism of your purpose. This is no different than the mandate regarding all advertising, marketing, sales, and business practices. For a small business to blindly adopt practices its owner observes used by big, dumb, public corporations with very different agendas and obligations, that employ Madison Avenue ad agencies with their own agendas, or for the owner to listen to the advice of big corporate CEOs or worse, academic theorists, about his business will more often make him road kill than successful. Modus operandi has to be congruent with chief objectives. The greatest saltwater-fishing champion in the world should not be trusted to advise the GM of an NFL football team on much of anything. The games are too different.

I mention NSA specifically because anybody poking around in "speaking," working at it professionally or just starting out, being seen speaking will inevitably be pointed to NSA. It will appear to be *the* place you are *supposed to* go: *the* organization you are *supposed to* join. In many respects, that's so. But they won't give you the caution label or the side effects list, so I have. Be circumspect.

CHAPTER 12

Call to Action and Closing the Sale

and How I Have Turned Terrified and Terrible

Platform Salespeople into Killer Closers

Who Make Millions Speaking-to-Sell

Brace yourself.

Buckle yourself in.

I am about to give you a *million-dollar secret*. It put over a million dollars in my pocket every year for many years and has done the same for many others who I've "coached up" on the secret. If you add everybody together, you can fairly call this a *billion*-dollar secret. It is even behind a company that rose from nothing to over a billion dollars a year in revenue. Today, I speak-to-sell on stage a lot less than at any other time in my life, but I often drive $100,000 to $1-million in sales via speaking in a live webcast or audio CD or video DVD sent to an "audience" and help others duplicate that feat—with the same secret.

If you get nothing else from this book, accepted nothing else from this book, but absolutely, thoroughly embrace and live by this million-dollar secret, you will be far, far, far richer, more powerful, and happier than you will otherwise be and than 95% of all other peers, colleagues, and competitors. You'll be happier because you'll be dealing with reality, instead of fantasy, which erases frustration. Most frustration comes from false expectations. You'll be more powerful because you will more frequently get what you want. You'll be richer because more people will more readily hand over more of their money to you.

This secret should be in a sealed envelope, hidden in a cave that you must brave snakes and fire and death traps to get into, like Indiana Jones going after the Holy Grail. It should require you to remove sword from stone. It should cost a hell of a lot more than whatever sum you paid for this book. I should get a least $10,000 to whisper it in your ear. We should have to wear trench coats and slouch hats and meet in an underground parking garage at midnight for the exchange, looking over our shoulders the entire time. But because I am *such* a generous fellow, here it is:

They must be told *exactly* what you want them to do.

They must be told to buy.

Given clear, precise, direct marching orders.

You won't think so.

There are three speakers I've seen—out of thousands, over forty years—who can get away with *not* delivering a pitch. Audiences are so enthralled; they stampede without being told and buy all that is available of the speaker's stuff to take home. The odds of you being the fourth member of this strange fraternity aren't good. I've seen hundreds of others think this is what should happen and fail miserably. Often, they take it personally. No, rejection's no fun—but it's almost always something you created, usually by your own bad ideas and behavior, like entitlement.

My friend Mike Vance, a creative thinking/living wizard and once personal associate of Walt Disney, was one of the three I've seen get away with no selling and still sell tons at the back of the room. He was magical. And people wanted more. But still, the times I had him speak to my groups, at my conferences, I stepped in and sold his resources for him and trumped the results he got when leaving it to just the magic.

It is the fallacy that so many presenters want to believe: *if I'm really good up there and deliver great information that is clearly beneficial, people will be smart enough to want what's next—I shouldn't have to browbeat them and intimidate them and "close" them.*

Your ego, your entitlement about this is your worst enemy.

Nuts. Jesus Christ invented the altar call. Oral Roberts perfected it.

Decide, as Zig put it, if you want to be a polite, poorly paid professional visitor or a highly paid professional salesman, behave accordingly. **Highly paid salesmen never leave buying up to the buyer. Master salesmen are master *closers*.**

In the advertising business, where I've also lived long and prospered, there is a thick dividing line between brand or image advertising and direct-response advertising. The first is largely immeasurable, rarely objectionable, and often beautiful and elegant. The latter is accountable, often pugnacious, and to some, offensive and often ugly. The first is genteel, the latter pushy and forceful. In speaking, the same differences exist between speaking and speaking-to-sell. It all starts with the purpose. The speaker never needs to "close" and therefore never needs to sense audience resistance and overcome it or get negative reviews afterward to upset his sensitive self-image. But if your purpose is to sell, *you will have to* close and close hard, and your purpose has to be *those* results—if need be, to the exclusion of all other results.

It has been about thirty years since I've permitted any organization I speak for to give out and collect comment forms or surveys, but I remember a two-day association event with many speakers where I got the most "A" and the most "F" grades of any. My audience split between loving and absolutely hating me. The haters' comments were all about my selling and hard closing. I also, by far, took the highest compensation home of any speaker, by about a six-figure margin, which was one of the two things I came to get. The other thing is the individual buyers to keep as customers going forward—and why would I want customers I had to tippy-toe around when it came to selling them the next thing I wanted them to buy?

Assuming you go to speak for a direct result—money or appointments for your business to produce money—you will need to close the sale of the goods or services or the appointment. And I also suggest doing it in a way that gives you the customers you can do something with, leaving behind those who strenuously object to being sold to. This is not about being loved by all. It is about extracting gold needles out of a haystack and leaving the hay behind.

How *do* you close the sale, from the front of the room or the stage, to a group, small or large?

In different venues, with different sizes and kinds of audiences, and with different propositions, the great closer's closing percentage varies. I've often sold to 70% to 90% in perfectly set-up situations, to 25% to 30% in less ideal circumstances. But there is no situation where a different *approach* is called for. Closing is closing: live or via webcast (where, incidentally, I have regularly been the "star" presenter, producing from $500,000 to $2 million per four-hour presentation for several years, for GKIC), twenty-five physicians in a three-hour preview seminar, 250 weight-loss buyers in a one-hour lunch 'n learn, or 2,500 in an association meeting, in seventy-five minutes. Closing is closing is closing.

Closing the sale one-to-many is pretty much the same as closing one-to-one. For that reason, I recommend reading or rereading books like *The Closers* and Zig Ziglar's *Secrets of Closing the Sale* and thinking about applying the techniques in them to speaking-to-sell.

Closing sales is about three things: appropriateness of prospects (audience), script, and attitude. We've discussed attitude a lot throughout this book, so here we'll zoom in on script. The script is built from tactics you choose for closing. One tactic must be precise instruction. "Here's what we're going to do now," and then you tell them. Let's back up and start at the start of the closing . . .

Usually, you need a bridge, from the content (information, education, entertainment) to the pitch: "Here's what I have for you to take home . . . " The bridge includes the reason-why for what you are going to offer, and that reason obviously has to be about the benefits to them, not about your payday. A version of the bridge script I used for many years is included at the end of this chapter as an example. Keep in mind I was selling multimedia information products. If you are selling a follow-up appointment with the sleep consultant at your mattress store or a paid or free introductory dance lesson or a forensic analysis of six months of the business owner's purchasing or whatever, a specifically appropriate bridge needs to be built. If you are selling a juicer, fitness gadget, water purifier, or other home product, the appropriate bridge needs to be built. Its insides differ, but the bridge architecture can be the same in any and every situation. Also keep in mind that your entire presentation is a sales presentation, but most won't and aren't supposed to realize it—instead, they are swept up and swept along in a presentation they feel is informational and motivational, which deposits them on the bridge.

Next in the script is the offer of goods or services or opportunity, appointment, exam, whatever. In it, you (usually quickly) describe each item in three parts: *what* it is (its features), *why* it is (problems solved, needs erased, desires fulfilled, benefits), and what it's *worth* (retail price and/or comparative value). If you are stacking items into a bundle, the established values stack, to then be discounted from. Which gets us to *presentation of price*, which can be done as (1) "retail" price/value, (2) discounts (for reason) to net price, (3) payment terms, if needed, (4) re-use of or final price minimization by apples-to-oranges comparison and/or by return on investment argument. If you haven't done it earlier, you'll next deliver the *risk-reversal promises and guarantee(s)*. Then, finally, as I said above, *instructions*: you tell them exactly what to do to buy or opt-in. This is usually pushed by *scarcity* or bonus gifts available in limited number to the first x-number.

To pedantically summarize as a checklist:

1. Bridge

2. What

3. Why

4. Worth

5. Price

6. Guarantee

7. Instruction

8. Scarcity

Now, the rookie or amateur mistakes.

One: *not* leaving yourself the necessary time to deliver this in full. Most speakers—especially if attitudinally averse to the selling—use up too much of their allotted time teaching, informing, motivating, and entertaining (a.k.a. being loved) and cheat the time left for selling (a.k.a. getting results), thus rushing it, appearing stressed, and ruining the whole thing. The selling isn't the thing you do with whatever time is left over. It's *the* reason you're there.

Two: *not* memorizing, practicing, and mastering the "pitch." If you are not going to script the entire speech and memorize it and deliver it verbatim and instead work from outline, talking points, prompted by a slide or object, and roam around a bit, that's your choice. It is ill advised, but a lot of speakers do it. But you still must memorize the "pitch" and be able to deliver it perfectly; with perfect timing; with practiced and perfected pace, timing, pause, inflection, and gesture, so when you move into it you have zero stress over remembering or forgetting, and it is, as Yogi put it, déjà vu all over again. With the "pitch" I lived on for about ten years, you could pick any point in it, give me a sentence, and I could go from there flawlessly, even if you woke me out of a dead sleep to do it. This is how Broadway theater actors perform the same role and script night after night after night and never forget lines or get flop sweat—like amateurs doing community theater in the high-school auditorium. You decide for yourself: amateur or pro?

How I Have Turned
Terrified and Terrible Platform Salespeople
into Killer Closers Who Make Millions Speaking-to-Sell

Yes, I have done exactly that a number of times. It's never been fun for the speaker or me. It's never been easy. But I have also never failed at it. There is, for this, quoting Stone, a "success system that never fails." In one case, I took a guy bombing in a venue where his predecessor had averaged $50,000 a speech. He was doing almost nothing. In six weeks, he was topping the $50,000. In another case, a woman who'd bombed on two occasions got her presentation retooled and, next outing, topped $100,000. I also took a financial advisor from booking free appointments with a pitiful 20% of his free workshop audiences to booking fee-paid appointments with 60%. Here is how it's done . . .

- **First, I invested a lot of time and effort getting the person past their internal, emotional inhibition and timidity about selling from the platform and at least worked on their bigger pile of emotional and belief system bullshit about money.** Odds are, there's a big blob of "stuff" between you and attraction of money, sort of an invisible, psycho-emotional obstacle course money's asked to fight its way through to get into your hands. It's *not* the money playing hard to get, *it's you!* And money has lots of other suitors to choose from. I know, I know, I know—this is *not* what you want to spend time on. You *just* want "the seventeen hypnotic words to say." You're probably impatient with all of my remarks about this throughout the book. And I don't blame you one bit. But I assure you, *this* is what makes it possible for you to wield the selling sword or leaves you powerless to even lift it.

- **Second, I imposed the discipline of a carefully crafted speech or seminar, designed to set up the sale.** Speakers want to be undisciplined. A lot of mediocre salespeople want to be undisciplined, too. Most broke people are broke because of a lack of discipline imposed on self and work—*not* because of lack of opportunity.

- **Third, I imposed the even tougher discipline of a word-for-word script for the bridge and the offer,** memorized, and delivered verbatim, until it is "old-shoe" comfortable to the speaker.

- **Fourth, I installed practice and conditioning.** The speaker should (A) read the scripts aloud; (B) practice in front of a mirror; (C) practice with video and video playback; (D) record it perfectly then listen to it at least daily for a month, while driving, mowing the lawn, or walking the dog; and (E) get a sleep learning player and pillow speaker, and let it play (barely audibly) all night for a month. Ideally, also, (F) go deliver it at least several times where it doesn't count, and work out the kinks. That's why *pro* football teams scrimmage during the week, with the game plan and scripted plays they intend using on Sunday.

- **Fifth, I crafted the offer itself, to be as interesting and irresistible as possible.** The best closer alive can't be effective with a bad thing to sell. For example, a "free exam" is vanilla and uninteresting. "The Most Thorough

Wellness Exam Of Your Life"—from which "These Seven Vital Questions Will Be Answered" is more interesting. A "satisfaction guarantee" is vanilla and mundane. A "bottom of the jar guarantee" where you can use the entire month's supply and "if you don't wake up every morning free of stiffness, aches, and pains and feeling ten years younger" you can return the empty jar for a full refund, is a lot better. One bonus is better than none, but five are a lot better. Something they'll lust for is better than something they need.

- **Sixth, I took pains to put the speaker in front of "high probability audiences," who were a good fit with what he or she had to sell.** As I mentioned elsewhere in this book, the "instructors" of our "crime safety classes" were certain to get better results with an audience of women real estate agents in an area where a serial rapist attacking women agents at empty homes was on the loose and in the news than an audience of women in general at a civic club luncheon. Or with late-shift nurses at a hospital, who had to walk alone through a dark parking lot at night, than office tower secretaries who left work in daylight at 5:00 p.m. A chiropractor speaking to country club members about flexibility and how it can improve their golf swing has a better shot at success than speaking to a general audience at the Elks Club.

Ultimately, success at speaking-to-sell is about *confidence.*

Confidence is boosted by competence. Confidence is boosted by having a well-crafted, effective speech to deliver. Confidence is boosted by having a sales pitch that works. Confidence is boosted by practice to the point of déjà vu delivery. You can build all that for yourself or hire an expert at this to assist you. Ultimately, confidence is boosted by certainty—reducing the question from "Win or lose today?" to "How much will we win by?" It's a closed feedback loop, too. Confidence grows with successful experience, a good reason to deliver the same speech and pitch over and over again, not a new, untested one each time. If you must vary the speech to different audiences for best results, it should be by exchanging modules but still keeping intact 100% of the architecture, nearly 100% of the time allotments to each piece and pace, 70% of the content, and 99% of the pitch. Otherwise, you swap confidence for anxiety, and anxiety is expensive.

There is real, authentic confidence. There is fake, ginned-up, empty confidence. My friend Nido Qubein, now president of High Point University, and a highly polished but still "killer" platform sales pro, says, "Motivation without foundation only produces frustration." The neuro-linquistic programming idea of "putting yourself in a state" is only valid if there is a solid foundation of competence underneath the mind play. If you take ginned-up confidence into a gunfight, with no gun, or absent the will to pull the trigger mercilessly, you die. As Glenn W. Turner said, "You want to be the bullfighter with steak sauce on his sword—but that's best if you are also an extremely competent bullfighter."

I started my business life trying the ginned-up, hyper-motivation-based confidence. It was popular in 1970, it's popular now. All the energy yells, the hot-coals-walking, the affirmations and visualization, Peale's positive thinking, the metaphysicians' manifestation, all of it is just hot air if it is not coupled with competence. And if you have to choose one versus the other, choose competence. Confidence can't produce competence, but competence can produce confidence. Speakers, particularly speakers who sell but also all performers, live and die by confidence, so it seems—but the ones who thrive are confident because they actually know what they are doing up there. They are not hoping for desired reactions; they know how to force them. No magician ever actually lets anybody "pick a card, *any* card." He uses what's called a "force" to compel and ensure a predetermined outcome, so he can be incredibly calm and confident (even if faking nervousness and uncertainty).

I'm going to make a statement now that is both braggadocio and largely unwelcome. It has to do with *mastery*. My friend Chris Cardell says the biggest difference between rich and un-rich is mastery versus what he calls *dabbling*. I *mastered* selling from the platform. Tom Hopkins, Zig Ziglar, a few others, out of thousands of speakers, mastered it too. Warren Buffett mastered selecting companies to invest in—by a formula of his own divining. Donald Trump mastered "the art of the deal" and self-promotion—by formulas of his own divining. Walt Disney mastered the dynamic retelling of old, known fairy tales—by formula of his own divining. If you examine any top achiever at anything, you will find mastery and formula. You may be able to suit your purposes—if small—by dabbling at speaking or speaking-to-sell and by "loose" approaches to it. But if you want top results, you'll commit to mastery with formula.

Dan Kennedy's Speaking-To-Sell "Bridge Script"

Well, we've covered a lot of territory and you have awareness, information, and opportunity you did not have ___ minutes ago. But there are *problems*. I'm going to take about ___ minutes to identify them and solve them—guaranteed.

First, there's the way our minds work: not very well. Forty-eight hours from now you won't remember my name or most of what I said, and if you try hard to think about it, you'll find yourself confused. Seventy-two hours from now you'll only remember a joke. Five days, you won't even remember—*being here.* <laugh>. Our minds *are sieves:* in the top, out the bottom. New information can only be accepted, understood, and used through repetition and immersion. It takes twenty-one nights in a new home before your hand automatically goes to the light switches in the dark. So, that's problem number one: memory. Oh, and if you scribbled notes like a madman, odds are those notes are going to the same place all the other notes have gone from all the other seminars—boxes in the garage or basement, *never* to be seen again. <laugh>

Second, there's the trouble with ideas and information. That's not enough. That's the failure of even a great day like this one. Ideas and information without application and implementation only create frustration and have no value. You need *tools*. Information about farming is useless without a tractor. If you go home from today, from these _____ minutes you just spent with me, *you wasted your time!* If you go home with new ideas about farming but no tractor, you've got nothing. Others may be okay with wasting your time and taking home their paycheck. I am not.

Now, *good* news. I've figured this out. I have *tools* for you to take home and actually, almost *instantly*, use to get results, to get money. I'm also going to send you home with what you need for repetition and immersion. But most importantly, unlike any other speaker, I'm sending you home with a *tool kit* you can use right away. And I'm going to guarantee it: not just your satisfaction with it but your results from it. So, let me quickly tell you about my two guarantees, then the resources and tool kit that I am sending you home with . . .

CHAPTER 13

Peer Pressure

Putting people under peer pressure to buy works.

Peer pressure has put smartphones and iPads in an awful lot of hands, driven people onto Facebook and LinkedIn. *If you're not there, you're square.* In an earlier chapter, I talked about the false presumption that people act on the free will given as birthright or that they act rationally. Not long ago, I was having a "catching up" phone call with an old client and friend with whom I hadn't spoken in several years. He expressed fresh curiosity and obvious, wistful envy of my absolute refusal to use the Internet— thus no email and no social media for me. He talked of hanging out with a top neuroscientist who explained that the constant connectivity to all the devices and the world inside them is literally reprogramming the human brain, that this is engineered to be addictive in much the same way as slot machines and video games. He said that the demands on his time made by his involvement with social media seemed to be worsening, with no improvement in his business to show for it. He confessed his impotence to me as a patient might to a doctor. I told him it reminded me of the ancient joke: guy tells doctor, "It hurts like hell when I lift my arm up this way," and the doc says, "Then don't do that." I told him: you are a millionaire, you have a large income from a business that is not—itself—dependent on all this stuff, you have prominence, many people are eager to involve themselves with you, so why don't you just refuse to continue having more and more of your life taken over by all this connectivity and obligation that is making you so stressed and miserable?

His answer, summarized, was that most of the people he hangs with would think him a dinosaur, an idiot, an entirely unreasonable SOB, or all three, were he to refuse to communicate by email or LinkedIn, exit Facebook, stop texting, etc. His answer reveals incredible emotional insecurity. I pointed out that people certainly thought these same things about me, and, as far as I was concerned, they could kiss my ass. He, a wealthy adult man, is just as controlled by peer pressure as an emotionally fragile thirteen-year-old girl desperate for acceptance by her peers.

This is not limited to the Pavlovian process Apple has relied on in recent years to sell its stuff—starting with long lines of people camping out overnight to be first into the stores when the new gizmo is first available. This is why new movies have gigantic box office takes on their opening weekends: people don't want to be the ones who haven't seen it, when their peers have. The post-World War II boom in consumerism was entirely driven by peer pressure, termed, in advertising circles, as "keeping up with the Joneses." A new car parked in one driveway on the street instantly rendered everyone else utterly unhappy with their dependable jalopies they'd been perfectly satisfied with the day before. I have clients who are adults in their forties, fifties, and even sixties paying upward of $200 for "fashion jeans" with holes ripped in them and faded spots put in as if bleach accidentally spilled on them, so that they can fit in with younger entrepreneurs in our crowd. I would be embarrassed to show up at the stables to shovel shit out of the stalls wearing these things—they are at seminars, showing them off. *Were it not for peer pressure, would*

any of them, entirely of their own free will and judgment and preference,
choose to buy and wear ripped and soiled pants? No.

In speaking-to-sell, we have grand opportunity to apply peer
pressure for our purposes. The single biggest benefit of putting
people into a physical environment with four walls, preferably one
exit, you on stage, peers seated all around each person, is your ability
to create and impose peer pressure to drive sales. By well-conditioned
habit, they all look around at each other to see how they should
respond.

This is why no distance method—tele-seminar, webinar, etc.—
ever works like the actual butts in seats, bodies in room, speaker
on stage method. You can replicate just about everything but the
peer pressure. You can mimic it and claim it, like they do on QVC
with the running order tally and countdown clock, or some online
marketers do, with buyers' tweets about their decision to buy instantly
retweeted. But you can't replicate the effect of real people in a real
room seeing people around them respond, jump up, run to buy, then
unwrap and love the package they bought. Who has the courage
to pass the collection plate in church without putting anything in
the plate, when everybody passing the plate toward him is putting
money in, the person on the other side of him waiting to be handed
the plate is watching him? Who wants to *visibly* be the odd man out?

Many speakers like using trial closes. If you've ever seen my
friends Tom Hopkins or Ted Thomas work, you've seen masters at
eliciting a series of yes-responses from audiences. It may feel uncomfortable to you observing it and may be uncomfortable for some in
the audience, and it is "old school," but for the confident speaker,
it is a powerful tool. At some point, the audience realizes they are
being had, but there's not much they can do about it, and if they're

in a good mood and it's done good-naturedly, they'll play along and, each trial close will get more hands or hollered yesses than the one before, until, ultimately, they've all pre-agreed to buy before the real close. This practice dates all the way back to the traveling "medicine show" hucksters gathering crowds and selling while standing on the back of their horse-drawn wagons. You'll be unlikely to find a get-rich-in-real-estate speaker anywhere in the world not using it today. But it also works in more "sophisticated" environments, with all sorts of audiences. It works because of peer pressure. As hands go up, the other hands around them go up. And yes, the physical act of giving in and raising hands affects the mental and emotional state. Being part of the excited hand raisers actually triggers endorphin release and feels good, so the next time, they're quicker and more eager to do it, and the next even quicker and more eager.

A secondary form of peer pressure is use of testimonials. Live, in-person testimonials—carefully controlled—can be very powerful. In a seminar that sells financial advisors into leaving their present firms and affiliating with my client's company, we had a mastermind meeting for top-income advisors with that company going on in a separate room, and at a predetermined time paraded them in for a panel discussion for the potential recruits, where they were each quickly interviewed on stage about their income, experience with the client, original skepticisms and concerns, and present love for us all. If you are making $100,000 and would dearly love to make $250,000, and you hear from a parade of folks making $500,000 to $2-million who all tell you the same thing—the firms you're presently affiliated with are dead weights tied to your ankles holding you back, but affiliation with this firm unlocks the chains and sends you soaring—that's desired peer pressure. I've had cosmetic surgeons, chiropractors, dentists, business opportunity marketers, and many others use live-and-in-person testimonials at their group presentations. Next best, video clips. Next best, letters dramatically read and dramatic success stories dramatically told. I would never deliver a speech to sell without incorporating testimonials as proof and as peer pressure.

Live peer pressure can be visual too. For a number of clients who sell event attendees into coaching programs, we've put the existent coaching clients into special sports jackets or other apparel so that, scattered throughout the audience, they create a visible "in" crowd vs. outsiders, winners vs. losers, cool kids' club vs. outsiders pressure. When I structure multi-hour sales seminars, I want the main selling done before a break but not at the end, so buyers return to their seats with their new "toy box" and happily look through it and ooh-and-aah over it, sitting right between two pour souls with no toy box. I want to refer to something in the toy box as if everybody had it. "Look, real quick, at the example on page 46 of your big blue notebook." On the next break, a bunch of intimidated, frustrated, deprived folk will rather sheepishly hurry back to get their toy box.

As a speaker, you want to use all the "group dynamics" you can to further your cause. At GKIC events where we have long-time members mixed with new members, I like to establish authority by asking all those with us for five years, ten years, fifteen years; those who traveled from distant foreign lands; and—most importantly—those having invested over $100,000 on our resources over their tenure to stand. The last demo creates peer pressure to invest in resources when offered. Often, our top-level members have discount vouchers in their pockets requiring being among the very first buyers of any offered resources, so at the close by the speaker, they are moving; they are already known as our top dogs, so "follow the leaders" literally draws others up out of their seats and brings them back to the product tables.

WHICH GETS ME TO THE STAMPEDE.

Stampedes feed on themselves, enlarge by themselves. It only takes a few to draw in many. A good speaker who sells knows how to start a stampede, to buy or sign up for whatever he's offering. He uses scarcity, limited bonuses, specific instruction, often even his own "pied piper" physical movement to get people up and moving. Almost without exception, a few moving cause more to move and they cause more to move. If you could hover over the whole thing and get an aerial view, you'd see a person rising in aisle #7, seventeen seats in, rise, move, and almost immediately the guys in the same row, from twenty-one and nine seats in, stand and start moving, then a guy in the next row forward, then . . . and so on.

I have been told, "Well, you won't create a stampede here, with our people." Always wrong. I was told that the first time I spoke to a supposedly prim and proper audience in England. I was told this about a big dental conference—but I had dentists stampeding so wildly they knocked down and stepped on several people. One of them got a broken finger. I was told this about the convention of the American Society of Training and Development—but our speaker sent hundreds stampeding out of the auditorium and down the aisle of the exhibit hall, knocking down booth displays on either side, crazed, to get an offered, free audio cassette.

Here's an important way to think about all this: most speakers put all the weight of winning or losing on their own shoulders, but that's not necessary or advisable. Others can do some of the heavy lifting for you—by the way they are dressed up and seen, recognized from the stage, interviewed on panels—and can act as your show ponies in various ways. Others can be "fire starters" that get everybody else ablaze. A few can be "set up" to start the stampede effect.

Speaking-to-sell is about a lot more than the speech and the speaking.

CHAPTER 14

No Compunctions

Comedians talk about "killing" an audience, jokes that "kill," a good show as one where "I killed."

In my book *Make 'Em Laugh & Take Their Money*, I talk more about the very confrontational nature of stand-up comedy. Without appearing on the attack—in most cases—comedians have to take control, manipulate, dominate, *master* an audience. They do not view the sought-after audience response as optional. It's not up to the audience whether or not to find them and their material funny—they set out to *make* the audience find it funny.

A successful speaker has the very same attitudinal approach. You intend that they are putty in your hands. And when selling, you intend they buy. That's not up to them to make a considered decision about. You intend, as Glenn Turner put it, to reach into their jackets and purses and take the money right out of their wallets. You are not interested in giving them a choice in this matter. You are trying, by psychological manipulation, control, peer pressure, or sheer force of your will to force them to buy. Any compunction about doing that is deadly.

Have you ever played the stare-down game? You sit across from someone, get nose-to-nose, stare, and whoever blinks first loses. This, to me, is what platform selling is about. Incredible concentration, force of will, and control of energy to make them blink—that is, surrender and buy. They can start out arms folded with a skeptical stare, uncomprehending with a blank stare, or even determined not to respond at all with a disapproving stare. Doesn't matter. I will break their will and make them blink. When I hit that stage, I'm going out there to *kill.*

I developed this when speaking-to-sell in bad environments with bad audiences, like with eight real estate agents who didn't want to be in their office's compulsory sales meeting, hungover, still half-asleep, one or two reading the newspaper, all checking watches. Or some breakfast networking group, where speakers don't customarily sell anything, and doing so instantly raises hackles. I did a whole lot of that. And I needed to go into those places and walk out with some-body's money in order to eat, so I quickly set aside all compunctions, conditioned myself to be unaffected by anything and everything, and go in for the kill. It is better not to be literally speaking for food, but it does sharpen your intent.

I did well over 150 of these miserable gigs over about eighteen months and walked out empty-handed only three times—and I still remember the details of all three. At the other 147, I got into some-body's wallet.

One of the pump-up things I listened to while driving to these gigs was Bobby Darin singing "Mack The Knife": "Oh, the shark bites with his teeth, dear, and he keeps them pearly white; but old Macheath, dear, has a knife and he keeps it outta sight." I also listened to Zig: "They've got my money in their kitchen drawer, I've got their cookware out in my car and I ain't leaving 'til we make the exchange." In these early days, I was pretty clumsy and primitive about my selling from the front of the room, but I was ruthless and determined, so I was effective enough to grind out over $100,000 the first year.

You may not want to hear this, but even as I've gotten much, much, much more sophisticated at this, ruthlessness still plays a vital role. These days, I have no financial need and it is a lot harder to get myself into the state of really, profoundly wanting their money to the exclusion of every other thought, but when I do, I still *kill.*

CHAPTER 15

How to Bomb

Lay an egg. Bomb. Flop. (Where the term "flop sweat" came from.) Be ridden out of town on a rail. Slink away, tail beneath one's legs. *Die* up there.

Ugh.

I hate not doing well—Howie Long ripping off locker doors and chewing on them kind of hate not doing well. Throwing things, cussing, angry hate not doing well. In a funk, not to be messed with, big black bear with acid reflux and sore feet and hemorrhoids hate not doing well. Eyes gone demonic red hate not doing well.

Bombing is not one of my favorite things. You may not hate it as much as I do—although I think you can measure somebody's sincere commitment to success at something by how much they hate failing at it, and that's worth thinking about—but I can promise, you *won't like it much.*

Bombing, for me, is not selling—nothing else. And I have, any number of times, not bombed in performance terms, yet bombed in selling results. I've had audiences seem into me, happy, laughing, crying, clapping, but with wallets kept clenched way up inside their butt cheeks. Well, I don't give a rat's patootie about all the other stuff. So, poor sales, I bombed.

Because I hate it so much, I've given it a lot of thought. And I have gotten great clarity about why I bomb, on the relatively rare occasions I do bomb. It has to do with being an idiot, repeating the same known mistake but expecting different results. My stupidity and pain may be instructive. It did not require years on a therapist's couch or a little herd of consultants and coaches to figure it out. It was patently obvious.

Every time I have bombed—without exception—thinking way back and thinking about a very recent unsatisfactory gig, where $11,000 was sold but $50,000 should have been, one of two factors, or both, were responsible: one, the source and nature of the audience—meaning, I was in front of the wrong people; two, I delegated or ceded control over things affecting the outcome and wound up working against headwinds, in disadvantageous circumstances. Every darned time. I strive to avoid these two black holes and urge you to do the same. And, since I'm still imperfect at it, as dear old Dad said: do as I say—not as I do.

The first thing you *don't* want to do is get in front of the wrong audience. Or even a poorly prepared audience. The great comedian Shelley Berman told me—and told his audiences—"I'm doing the same act all week, with five different audiences. How well I do *tonight* has a lot more to do with you than with me." Of course, you never want to shuffle off responsibility to customers or make excuses for poor results, because that robs you of the thing you need most, control. But why would the same speech delivered the same way (and inspected on video to verify that it was) sell $100,000 worth of stuff to one audience but lay an egg with another? Who is in that room makes a big difference. It is vital to go where you best fit, to speak to audiences appropriate for you, with high probability of receiving you well. Trying to convert a town full of Hindus to Christianity may be a spiritually admirable mission, but you'd better not have your food and housing dependent on how many premium-priced, gold-gilded Bibles you sell to the group.

Personally, I need real business owners with brick-and-mortar stores, restaurants, and offices, small manufacturing firms, professional practices, and/or sales professionals who have to prospect and get face-to-face and nose-to-nose. I need them to have sincere ambition. That means, for example, if I'm in a room with a bunch of people who have only web sites and think they have businesses and think of themselves as "Internet marketers," or I'm in a room with a bunch of people who've been put there by employers or sales managers rather than by their own motivation, I'm in trouble. You have to know whom you need in your room. Beyond that is the issue of how well prepared they are. Big-name comedians like Seinfeld, Ron White, Louis Black, etc. always do well now because the audience is well prepared in advance to find them hilarious and react appropriately. They **know** these guys are funny. The question is: what does the audience need to *know* in advance about you? Then, you'd better make sure they know it. Finally, for me, my best results are going to come with audiences who are not shocked or annoyed by, at certain point, being sold something. When I'm the first and only speaker a group has ever had sell to them from the stage at their association or corporate meeting, I have gotten results and usually can get results if they are otherwise the right audience, if they've been otherwise well prepared, and if that day I am very determined—because, even if up to that point they've been with me, laughing, clapping, agreeing, having a good time and it's been happy sailing, when they realize they're being sold something, the room suddenly chills and the sailing turns to slogging through knee-deep mud. Selling to trained buyers is a lot better for me, and there are plenty of those speaking opportunities, so why would I accept any others? Because, occasionally, I'm an idiot—only occasionally.

Anyway, that's the audience I know I can do well with—business owners with study ethic and work ethic, with real businesses, who aren't looking for the mythical easy button, but have sincere ambition to be and do a lot better. You need to know what audience you can do well with.

There is also what I call the "Passion Index." Different people have high passion and low passion for different things. Many people have low passion for information and behavioral change for health and wellness until they are diagnosed with a serious disease. For some years, I had an interest in a company that sold personal safety products via speakers giving classes. The passion for this went way up when there was a crime wave, an assault, or a serial rapist in the news. And we sent our team in wherever, whenever such a gift was provided to us. Ideally, you want to be speaking to an audience with relatively high passion for what you have to say and offer *and* be shrewd and calculating about linking what you have to say to their high passion. When speaking to sales professionals about my *Magnetic Marketing System®*, I could speak about making a lot more money as a sales pro *or* about eliminating "cold" prospecting, once and for all. The second ranks higher on the Passion Index for most salespeople than does the first. A long-time client of mine with a hugely successful martial arts academy business could speak about self-defense and martial arts mastery or about peak fitness, but he discovered the most persuasive thing to speak about is "How to Have Safer, Smarter, More Respectful Kids."

Next, the matter of control. Your presentation does not occur in a vacuum. There is the site, the room, appearance, layout, lighting, temperature, its safe isolation or its exposure to the jackhammers at an adjacent construction site or a marching band's practice across the hall, the stage, the sound, the A/V, the seating, whatever is occurring before you speak, whoever introduces you, the introduction itself, not having your time cheated by starting late, and on and on and on—plus, as already noted, whatever is supposed to be done and whatever actually gets done to properly prepare the audience for you in advance. You cannot accept the idea that *any* of this is outside *your* control. This is why, in recent years, I not only make many clients put meetings in my home city, where I can sleep in my own bed, keep my regular morning routine, and not be stressed or inconvenienced by travel, but I also make them put the meetings in my choice of hotel, where I have Kennedy-trained its staff and I control the physical arrangements, and use my A/V crew, also Kennedy-trained to meet my needs. Of course, I was not always able to impose such requirements, and you probably won't be able to, either. The only sane approach, then, is extremely negative and cynical: it is to assume *everybody* is either a moron or engaged in a sinister conspiracy to screw up your opportunity, cannot be trusted about anything as mundane as having a floor beneath your feet, delegate nothing without micro-supervision, and gird yourself for a fight over much to get it all as you need it to be. You have to determine exactly how everything needs to be, make that clearly known, then trust no one but yourself to see that it happens.

Please don't shoot yourself by classifying this as "negative thinking" you want no part of because you believe in the "power of positive thinking" or fear jinxing things. Leave your religion and superstition out of it. Your *neck* is on this line. If you must parachute jump, its best to know how the chute is to be packed and at least inspect it and probably better to pack your own chute altogether and get a skilled jumper to check your work.

Often I get to work with consummate pros in my same business who get it and have surrounded themselves with support folks who get it. When working for Chris Cardell in the UK, this is the case. He speaks as I do and shares the same level of understanding about the sum total of a lot of little things having major impact on outcome. He can be trusted to prepare and deliver a terrific introduction. The event management team he uses there—a company called Penguins—has the best people I've ever worked with anywhere, in all my years at this. Chris knows how to pick a site, stage a site, and create the best atmosphere. And he brings in an ideal audience. With Chris, I could just show up five minutes before going on with no worries. I wouldn't, but I could. Unfortunately, his audiences are all on the other side of an ocean I'm loathe to cross. And he is the rarest of birds. Even many people who speak, who put on conferences a lot, who should be as smart and as trustworthy about all this as Chris, are not. Not even close.

The A/V crew that traveled with us on the giant SUCCESS events, held mostly in basketball arenas, with audiences upward of 15,000, really knew their stuff. Setting up for our event was akin to setting up for a KISS concert. These were top pros. And they worked with me twenty-five to twenty-seven times a year, for nine years. I gave the same speech and did everything the same way every time. They liked me, too. Still. It's *my* $100,000 payday at stake, and in jeopardy if any of them forget or neglect anything. So, each and every time I went to them an hour ahead of my presentation to go over the checklist. If I can't trust them, you can't trust the volunteer chairman of the Sherman Oaks Elks Club or the guy setting up the meeting room at the Holiday Inn.

Ultimately, you make one of two choices about all this: you can gamble on what should be and be assured of somebody to blame and some nifty excuses for poor results afterward, or you can prevent all the sabotage in advance and give yourself the best possible opportunity but, of course, full responsibility too.

For the record, money is repelled by casualness and entitlement. Money flows to people who have great clarity about every detail of their performance of their skill and service and take nothing affecting it for granted.

CHAPTER 16

Meeting Planner Management

I f you are not filling your own seats with your own audiences, you will have *bureaucrats* to deal with—whether the chairwoman of the Ames, Iowa, Civic Club, where you are speaking for free to promote your local taxidermy shop, or the executive director and his minions of the National Association of Pig Whisperers, where you are being paid a fee to speak (but also selling product). You can see this relationship go awry in a scene in the movie *The Great Buck Howard*.

These people will often agree to anything verbally, then change everything with impunity. That's why you have a contract or at least a detailed confirmation letter, even with the nice little old lady running the Ames, Iowa, Civic Club. And you have a copy in your pocket to swing like a baseball bat if you must. A copy of a typical letter of confirmation for a speaking engagement appears at the end of this chapter. This example is about a "5" on a scale of "1" (loose) to "10" (super tight). This letter went to a long-time, trusted, and smart client, so I left a few items and some legalese out, but it'll give you the idea: describe exactly what you require to be effective. In writing. I do have much longer and detailed contracts, fully detailing what is and isn't acceptable in the meeting room, acceptable and prohibited behavior by the host, etc., right down to: "The room cannot have columns." This is not prima donna stuff, like requiring an exotic brand of water or only red M&Ms in the green room. This is about your selling opportunity. *Your* selling opportunity. So it's up to you to prevent anybody accidentally or intentionally screwing up that opportunity.

There are three kinds of meeting planners: well intended but dumb; liars, who agree to everything with no intention of honoring anything; and deliberate saboteurs, jealous of you and on their own egotistical power trip. Doesn't matter if they run you over with their car on purpose, taking dead aim and flooring it, or back over you by accident. Either way, you're maimed or dead. Don't let them.

If you are going to speak with any objective other than amusing yourself and, hopefully, basking in the glory of applause, you need to protect your ability to achieve that objective. This makes the getting of the gig *the beginning of* a management process over which anxiety and paranoia is appropriate—*not* an accomplishment. You must never let anything be "loose," to be "worked out later," or let any "oh, I'm sure that will be all right" assurances replace definitive agreement. By the way, just about the time I think I've seen every stupid thing that can be done to screw me, some meeting planner or emcee invents a new one.

Never expect what *you* don't inspect and verify. All of this also needs to be reviewed on site, with powers that be and any new players in any way affecting what you're doing—like host or emcee, A/V crew, etc. You need to check out the room to ascertain it is or will be set up for you per your instructions. You need to get what isn't right fixed. Don't be a baby about this. I would rather be thought of by somebody as difficult or annoying or high maintenance or a bully and leave with a giant sack of money than thought of as a nice, amiable, go-along-to-get-along fellow who leaves with an empty sack. Call me anything you like except late for dinner.

Many if not most speaking opportunities are one-time shots. If you don't get the result you need, they don't reassemble the audience for you tomorrow and give you a second chance.

WIN OR DIE

Once upon a time, gladiators and lions were pitted against each other for kings' amusement. The game was *win or die.*

If you had to achieve certain sales from a speech or be put to death, would you manage these matters differently than you do absent the death penalty? Well, if the gig's not important enough to manage everything affecting its outcome as if it were life and death, my advice is to skip it altogether and invest your time and energy in something important. Play to win, or don't play at all.

I *hate* people who are casual and lackadaisical about their jobs. If that's you, I consider you a dishonorable, slothful, irresponsible, foolish person deserving failure and misery. This is something not said enough to everybody. Some people deserve to starve. Not get ninety-nine weeks' unemployment, food stamps, free medical care, *and sympathy.* Starve.

EVERYTHING MATTERS

Environment matters: room setup, temperature—which needs to be and stay "too cold"—look and layout of the stage area, lighting, sound. If people can't see or hear, they aren't going to buy.

Audience preparation in advance of the speech matters—what you work to have them know about you, read by you, watch online, etc., so you need this kind of media, and you need to do whatever it takes to get them in front of the audience before you get in front of the audience. You want to be "pre-established" as an Authority and as a Celebrity. These are two of the three "Levers of Power" for a speaker (the third is Speaking or Speaking-to-Sell Skill).

Your introduction matters. You want to discourage or, if you can, prohibit freelancing. Let your introducer dazzle with his "three men walk into a bar" on his own time and dime. You should script it.

Sales choreography matters. You have to decide on and dictate when and how forms are handed out, where product is put to be dispensed (back of the room, *not* down the hall).

Give yourself every advantage.

Typical Letter of Confirmation for a Speaking Engagement

DAN S. KENNEDY

SPEAKING AGREEMENT: Between Kennedy Inner Circle, Inc. providing Dan Kennedy, Speaker (hereinafter: Speaker) and XXXXXXXXXXXXXXXXX (hereinafter: Client)

SPEAKING: This will confirm a 2017 speaking engagement on XXXXXXX, from 11:00 A.M. to 2:30 P.M., on subject matter re. competitive differentiation, marketing to affluent, price strategy, etc., specific details to be agreed on by Speaker and Client. May include one or two presentations and/or Q&A. Location: Crowne Plaza Hotel, Independence, Ohio. ANCILLARY SERVICES: (a) Speaker will provide a collection of sales copy re. the presentation for promotional purposes, and authorizes use of Name, Likeness, Credentials, Story, Content Descriptions, etc., subject to approval by Consultant to protect accuracy. Client may also use excerpts of up to one chapter or ten pages from any of the Speaker's books. (b) Speaker will publicize event to readers and constituencies he reaches via newsletters and other means, to the best of his ability, with no warranty of any specific amount or type of promotion from Speaker. (c) Weather and auto availability permitting, Speaker will bring his "Dean Martin Rolls-Royce" and make it available for photo opportunity with event attendees, and Speaker will be available for such photo opportunity as early as 10:00 A.M. or as late as 4:30 P.M. on April 28, 2017.

FINANCIAL ARRANGEMENTS: SPEAKER FEE of XXXXX REDUCED TO XXXXX in consideration of locating in Speaker's Home City and pre-existing client relationship.

RESOURCES: a package or packages of complementary, relevant resources from the Speaker will be offered during the presentation(s)* to the attendees, with Client approval of offers. Order Form provided by Speaker. Orders processed and fulfilled by Speaker.

Speaker shall retain XX% of those gross revenues and remit XX% to Client, on the 61st day following shipment of goods to customers (to allow for refunds per guarantee).

PAYMENT: A Deposit of XXXXX is required to initiate agreement, then a deposit of XXXXX by January 15, 2017 (totaling a 50% deposit). These deposits are *non-refundable*, dates not subject to change or cancellation. Balance of fee is due on arrival, on site.

*Speaker shall control audience and direct them from end of his presentation to an area at rear of meeting room designated for acceptance of purchase forms and dispensing of resources.

AT EVENT: Speaker's A/V needs: large screen, ELMO or VISUALIZER image projector, lavaliere (*clip on*) microphone; projector in center of a 6' table (not a projector cart); three large pads on easels + markers; stool with high back. On stage: pitcher of unsweetened ice tea.

ADDITIONAL NOTICES: (1) In the event of illness or injury prohibiting Mr. Kennedy's appearance, he will exert every effort to provide a suitable substitute, but is not subject to liability for non-appearance. In event of acts of God, terrorism, airplane malfunction, or similar interference prohibiting Mr. Kennedy's appearance, he is not subject to liability for non-appearance.

(2) Mr. Kennedy's presentations are copyright protected, rights reserved. Any re-broadcast or productization of presentations requires separate agreement. (3) Mr. Kennedy offers no warranties regarding accuracy or efficacy of advice or

information provided. His presentation is for general informational purposes only. Client indemnifies Mr. Kennedy against claims by Client's audience members related in any way to ideas, information, or advice presented. (4) Under no circumstances can Mr. Kennedy be held liable by Client or parties related to Client in any way, for any reason, for an amount exceeding compensation paid by Client per this agreement. (5) For purposes of this agreement, vendor is Kennedy Inner Circle, Inc., furnishing Dan S. Kennedy as Speaker.

Please date and sign a copy and return it with your deposit check to Kennedy Inner Circle Inc., 15433 N. Tatum Blvd. #104, Phoenix, Az. 85032 (Fed Tax ID#: XX-XXXXXX)

___OK   DATE_____

SIGNATURE_____

_____

NAME XXXXXXXX

FOR XXXXXXXXXXXXXXXXXX

CHAPTER 17

Can One Great Speech Make You Rich?

When P.T. Barnum went broke late in life, he reassembled a fortune as a speaker, with a lecture based on lessons from his life, called "The Art of Money Getting." It is reprinted in full in a book on Barnum-style marketing by my friend Joe Vitale, *There's a Customer Born Every Minute*, which I urge reading. Napoleon Hill, known to many of you thanks to his book *Think And Grow Rich*, made his money for years after its first publication by creating and announcing one new lecture after another and working with promoters in different cities to fill rooms for it. In truth, it was basically the same lecture given new titles. In the early days of the modern speaking profession, people I came to know like Zig Ziglar, Cavett Robert, and Bill Gove were few in number, all making very good livings with but one speech each. Cavett said "It is easier to get a new audience than to get a new speech."

When I first heard that from Cavett, I thought it seemed lazy and uncreative. I soon realized he'd ingeniously summarized why so many speakers are broke and so few rich. The broke ones are endlessly creating. And perfecting. They think the business is the speaking. But it isn't. The money is in getting a lot of good speaking opportunities where you can deliver an effective speech. Having more than one effective speech is a distraction and a waste of time. It's a comfortable place to go hide and play, instead of doing the work of getting gigs. Also, assembling a speech that successfully, reliably sells is no easy matter. Assembling speech material is easy. But a speech that sells is hard. Once you have an automobile that runs flawlessly, day in, day out, rain, shine, locust attacks, hot, cold, why on earth would you start over building another car from parts? Go see the USA in your Chevrolet. Same thing with a speech that sells. Build it, then drive the hell out of it until the wheels fall off.

For about twelve years, I delivered the same speech selling my *Magnetic Marketing System*®, in a seventy-five- or ninety-minute version, more than six hundred times, with such repetitive precision that you could time me with a stopwatch again and again and within thirty seconds' variance, you'd find me on the same word, making the same gesture, at the same number of minutes in. Giving this speech directly made me well over a million dollars net each year and indirectly made me rich. Some years earlier, I'd built one two-hour speech for Foster Hibbard, who then delivered it in hundreds of seminars for doctors for a business that I owned, and a different two-hour speech for myself, for those same audiences, and from 1983 to 1987, those two speeches generated millions of dollars. I still have the notes I used every time I delivered that speech, typed out, marked up with different color highlighter pens. More recently, the speech I originally wrote for myself to sell my *Renegade Millionaire System*® was used more often by Bill Glazer to sell that same product and probably neared the half-million-dollar mark in revenue from his speaking. For myself and for others, I've built the One Speech, then they or I have driven it until the wheels fell off.

Keep in mind, these are speeches that sell, not just speeches. They are not even speeches with a commercial inserted, like traditional TV programs; they are more like infomercials, engineered with every word, every story, the entire speech a sales pitch. The audience usually doesn't perceive it as such, but that's what it is, and must be— somewhat in the same way that the most enduring success books of all time are actually hundred-plus page sales letters. Napoleon Hill had an advantage there, as he was an advertising copywriter by trade.

These kinds of speeches can be incredibly valuable *assets*. A tenet of my approach to and teaching about business is to distinguish between *marketing* (a *doing*) and the development of marketing *assets* (*owning*). The first creates income, the second creates equity and wealth.

A one-to-many presentation that works, delivered in a room to an audience, live, can often be tweaked and transferred to other media, like DVD, webinar, teleseminar, TV infomercial, and printed sales letters. The earliest infomercials were all either seminar speakers doing their thing or boardwalk slicer-dicer pitchmen doing their thing, while the cameras rolled. One of the hugely successful infomercials of this ilk that I had a lot to do with was Susan Powter's "Stop The Insanity," produced by the brilliant "Packy" McFarland. Master pitchmen like Ron Popeil and even George Foreman still make this approach work on TV today. Again, such a presentation can be a very valuable asset. It provides leverage via the multiplying power of media versus the severely restrictive limits of manual labor. The speech that sells converted to a sales letter that can be mailed with mind-numbing regularity to large, responsive lists can make you rich. I know of one in its twenty-eighth year in the mail. I had one we mailed every week for seven years.

Even early pitchmen figured this out. The infamous seller of goat testicles transplant surgery, Dr. John Brinkley, who I wrote about with coauthor Chip Kessler in our book *Making Them Believe*, used the power of his own voice and "fireside chats" on the radio to draw patients from all over America—most of whom had to travel by train to his clinic. He perfected his pitch and ability to pitch as traveling medicine-show peddler and later in speaking to small groups of prospective patients. Then he moved his pitch to media, with multiplying effect.

Mark Hughes was the first guy in MLM to take the hotel opportunity meeting into tens of thousands of living rooms simultaneously with live two-hour infomercials on cable TV, Sunday nights—jet fuel poured into his creation, Herbalife. Like Dr. Brinkley, Hughes learned to pitch and crafted the health part of his pitch selling a precursor product called Slender Now out of the trunk of his car, one to one and one to a few gathered around or in living rooms. He made a monster fortune moving it to TV. (Just as an aside, TV is still an infinitely bigger, faster, and more powerful multiplier than YouTube and all other online media combined. Ask my clients at Guthy-Renker or the folks at QVC. George Foreman's presentation for the countertop grill made him, personally, $100 million. Ed Slott, a financial planning "guru," has made a fortune by moving his hotel meeting room speech to retirees to PBS and then licensing his brand and fame to financial advisors all over the country.)

So, it is unlikely, in today's world, that one great speech can make you rich from just speaking. But such a perfected speech that sells treated as a marketing asset and adapted for other media, with reach multiplied by that media, most certainly can. Today, Mark Twain would need media. And he'd want it.

The Story of the $100 Million Dollar Speech

In 1870, a young foreign correspondent for the *New York Tribune* made a round-the-world trip. Enroute from Bagdad to Nineveh, on the banks of the Tigris River, a Turkish guide told him a story.

The correspondent, Russell Conwell, turned it into a lecture he delivered more than six thousand times—earning fees exceeding $8 million (inflation-adjusted to today's dollars, about $100 million). Had he been selling with the lecture a course or an investment he could have easily multiplied his fees tenfold. Conwell was, incidentally, the founder of Temple University. If you are interested in great speeches, you should procure a copy of his "Acres of Diamonds."

CHAPTER 18

On the Road Again, I Just Can't Wait to Get on the Road Again, Makin' Music with My Friends, Out There on the Road Again

THE INTERNET IS THE MAGNIFICENT ANGEL WHO BRINGS UNTOLD GIFTS AND THE GREAT SATAN WHO TAKES SO MUCH AWAY.

One of the things it has done is democratize information and entertainment, providing endless and overwhelming supply free and nearly free. By this, the profit in protected intellectual property is in free fall. Musicians are back out on the road in droves, making their money from manual labor, shows and concerts, and tours. Disney is by far the most profitable movie studio because its movies—like its TV, radio, print, and online media—are marketing, driving park attendance, merchandise sales, and licensing. I could continue with example after example.

As a speaker, you can walk in all three places. One, you can speak to drive customers into and drive revenue of one or more connected businesses that provide goods, services, or experiences that can't be price-destroyed by the Internet. Two, you can, by speaking, through live events, deliver an experience that many people still want, that can't be replicated with free online media. Yes, they can watch the concert on their mobile devices at Starbucks, but that is not the same as *being at* the concert. This puts professional speakers out there on the road just like Willie Nelson still is. Many are traveling more, traveling overseas more, and doing more live gigs than ever before in their careers, as they find themselves incapable of generating the income they want from their information products. Fortunately, I built the better mousetrap and I extracted substantial cash along the way by sale of equity, so I do not share their financial need. Still, one of my three biggest speaking paydays in 2015 required travel to London and two days of seminar work there. Third, you can use all the online media so destructive to price and profit of intellectual property product as effective, far-reaching broadcast media to make yourself famous to then attract audiences to see you perform in person. In essence, product has become another marketing medium rather than a profit center.

There is such a big difference between non-Internet media that was and the Internet media that is. With TV infomercials, for example, my client of about thirty years, Guthy-Renker, literally plucked Tony Robbins out of Holiday Inn meeting rooms and made him a household name and famous brand, in part creating a huge income for him from speaking, but at the same time making hundreds of millions of dollars through the direct sale of the packages of CDs, DVDs, and manuals on the shows. TV was a rising tide that lifted all the boats in the Tony harbor and made plenty of money for all parties concerned. YouTube videos do the exact opposite and, further, destroy the TV opportunity. You rarely see an intellectual property product infomercial these days, because the bleed-off to Amazon, eBay, others' sites via Google, and the enormous mountain of free content by the same person or at least in the same subject category online makes the economics of TV virtually impossible. As I write this, most of the infomercial industry is either about driving direct sales of proprietary cosmetic or ingestible products that have to be smeared on or swallowed or about driving product onto retail shelves. For the author-speaker to get an infomercial deal now is a miracle, and I doubt even Jesus Christ could pull it off profitably. Tony Robbins is a prime example of a made-by-TV celebrity speaker, and I doubt you'll see another one. However, earned media still exists, in the "old" media and in online media. Today, for example, giving a TED Talk and having it online for all to see free gets book deals and creates or lifts speaking careers for a number of people. There's no money from it, and, arguably there's investment, but it's proven as promotional media.

Bottom line, money is being moved further and further back, in a sequence of events, from the speaking and the speaker's use of media. But then, in a big, sweeping, closed loop, often, money has to be gotten by speaking, with audiences made by that entire sequence. In my world, this is principally done with the seminars, boot camps, conferences, and boutique mastermind events sold to the list of "fans" built, organized, fenced, and maintained by the entire sequence. The $100,000 to $250,000 net weekend is alive and well in this business.

You *can* use ability as a speaker who sells to sell via some online media, like live webcasts—if you have proprietary product, have or have access to an established audience or good email and mailing lists, have affiliates' support, and can orchestrate all the logistics. But again, the bleed-off is a significant factor. Your audience isn't locked inside four walls with you at the Hilton. They are online—where Google, Facebook, Amazon, eBay, etc. all beckon. And the open rates of email, generally, are worsening by the day. The need to be mobile compatible, and the costs and limitations that imposes, grows by the day. It is *not* easy. At the company I founded and still work with as an author, speaker, and "personality" as well as a marketing advisor, GKIC.com, we have been consistently successful three to five times a year for the last several years, formulaically, with what are called online "launches," each for a new info-product, most carrying $2,000 price tags, with the launch campaign culminating in three- to four-hour live webcasts in which I've performed in one role or another—including speaking, to a live studio audience or just to the camera. There are details to know and adapt to, but if you can speak-to-sell to a live audience, you can speak-to-sell to a virtual audience. It's worth noting, though, that most speakers and most businesses utilizing this approach have it feed people through the product sold into an actual, physical, live event or into a room of telemarketers, where the real money is made. If you are unfamiliar with the whole "information marketing industry," you can poke around starting at info-marketing.org, or with certain resources at GKIC.com/store.

With that sort of in its own box off to the side, if you are speaking or intending to speak for your suppers—and for the glory of it—today, you are most likely going to be hitting the road. This appeals to *some* speakers. They tie the business travel to vacations, bring spouses or have them meet them at the end of a tour, sightsee, and generally find it all exciting. I just about lived "out there" for almost two decades, and, for me, it lost its luster quickly. Today, within the United States., I refuse to fly but by private jet, and I still get a little queasy and grumpy anytime I head to the airport. I've structured my business to force *most* activities including speaking gigs and audiences to come to me, and I can and do say no to some opportunities requiring travel from home. But this is by its own nature an on-the-road business—increasingly so, thanks to the Internet's impact—so, as example, my schedule for the next year includes five trips to varied places to speak, and only one of them is a place I like going anyway.

The *best* piece of advice I have for you about the travel to work is: if you *must* go, make each round-trip as packed with productivity as possible. If you want to also play, bookend it, but make sure the business trip is packed with business. Years back, when I was still hustling for gigs, I tried never to speak anywhere without having invited and gotten a few meeting planners or others who might book me into that event as guests, so I was always showcasing at the same time I was speaking. I never spoke without selling, so I was always acquiring customers. I've always whale-hunted for clients. With the trip itself, I had clients or media interviewers or others meet me at airports during layovers and for private meetings over meals in the cities I had to visit. If I had empty hours in a hotel room, I had phone appointments set up. Every way I could, I used every minute, and I leveraged the travel on the client's dime for my many purposes. I've let up on myself a little now, but I still tend to pack productivity into each trip.

The second best advice I have for you about the travel to work is: get as much money out of it as you possibly can. Some speakers only speak, so they weigh making zero dollars at home against whatever they make on the road. I get paid $19,000 a day to consult with clients coming to me or on the phone, and via that, my copywriting, and my writing, I can average $10,000 a day at home. Many other part-time speakers have some version of the same scenario. The dentist who also speaks at state dental association meetings sacrifices income from dentistry the days he's gone speaking. You have to factor this in to your pricing, your business strategy, and your decision making. If I'm going to give three days to travel to and from a speaking gig and to the speaking, I'm at least $30,000 in the hole the first morning—and that has to be recovered *plus* satisfactory compensation and profit. Fees alone aren't enough; a "stew" of immediate and subsequent, back-end income is needed.

To quote Shelley Berman, "A hotel is a place with miniature soap, gauze-thin towels, and plastic-wrapped plastic glasses." I have had bad nights in Ritz-Carltons. I'm not a fan. Whether you are or not, believe me, there'll be a day when you won't be, and the time to use speaking to build a business de-linked from it is early, not late.

A Brief Afterword

Not long ago, to a group of writers, I said that I had literally *written myself into existence*, and that is absolutely true.

I also *spoke* a business empire into existence. It grew and expanded and evolved far, far beyond my speaking, yet it still gets half its life from the spoken word, the other half from the written word. I *spoke* (and wrote) a fortune into existence for myself and fortunes for several people closely associated with me in the business adventure spanning decades.

When you can step up in front of an audience and speak purposefully, persuasively, and confidently, you take and hold an enormous amount of *power*.

There are no other qualifications or permissions required. No one can hold you back or stop you. There are no licenses required and no bureaucrats to contend with. All barriers are in your mind or made of your own absence of action. There is *power for the taking*. Christianity is evidence and demonstration. Giant "movement-like" companies like Amway are evidence and demonstration. Steve Jobs reinvented consumer product launches by speaking and certainly demonstrated just how powerful such a single speaker and his presentation could be—in driving to retail. The majority of US presidents, especially those people remember and who had much impact, from both sides of the political spectrum, were purposed, persuasive, confident, often fiery and polarizing speakers—and those inept at this who ran against them were crushed.

There was a time when my becoming one of the highest paid, busiest, and most successful professional speakers was as improbable as a cockroach metamorphosing into an eagle. I stuttered, for several years almost uncontrollably. I was an introvert. When I did step in front of an audience, early on, I was frankly *awful*. But I'm proof this is all learnable craft and mind-set. And path to power it most certainly is. I have an incredible amount of autonomy and am reputed to be somewhat "difficult." I require business done with me on my terms, and I dictate those terms—have for many years—and it is all possible in substantial part because of these learned skills and mind-set.

For anyone who takes this seriously, this book is the beginning of a lot of soul searching, thought, strategic planning, and work. Not the end of anything. The beginning.

DAN KENNEDY

FOR MORE INFORMATION ABOUT THE MEMBERSHIP
ORGANIZATION, MAJOR INTERNATIONAL
CONFERENCES, AND PUBLISHING COMPANY CREATED
AND FUELED BY DAN'S SPEAKING, VISIT

GKIC.COM

FOR INFORMATION ABOUT DAN'S BOOKS, VISIT

NOBSBOOKS.COM

TO ORDER DAN'S BOOKS, GO TO
AMAZON.COM, BN.COM, OR 1-800-CEO-READ.

TO COMMUNICATE DIRECTLY WITH DAN KENNEDY,

DO NOT EMAIL THE ABOVE SITES, ANY
OTHER SITES, OR ANY SOCIAL MEDIA.

Mr. Kennedy does not personally use the Internet or
receive or respond to online communication.

CONTACT:

KENNEDY INNER CIRCLE INC.

15433 N. Tatum Blvd. #104

Phoenix, Arizona 85032

FAX 602-269-3113 (Preferred)

PH. MESSAGES 602-997-7707

CPSIA information can be obtained
at www.ICGtesting.com
Printed in the USA
BVOW11s1721310118
506850BV00018B/248/P